Other Kaplan Success with Words Books

Success with American Idioms
Success with Business Words
Success with Medical Words
Success with Words for the TOEFL

Related Kaplan Books

Access America's Guide to Studying in the U.S.A.
Kaplan/Newsweek Business School Admissions Adviser
Kaplan/Newsweek Graduate School Admissions Adviser
TOEFL
TOEIC

KAPLAN

Success with Legal Words

By Lin Lougheed and the
Staff of Kaplan Educational Centers

Simon & Schuster

Kaplan Books
Published by Kaplan Educational Centers and Simon & Schuster
1230 Avenue of the Americas
New York, NY 10020

Copyright © 1998 by Kaplan Educational Centers

All rights reserved. No part of this book may be reproduced or
transmitted in any form or by any means, electronic or mechanical,
including photocopying, recording, or by any information storage and
retrieval system, without the written permission of the Publisher,
except where permitted by law.

Project Editor: Julie Schmidt
Cover Design: Cheung Tai
Interior Page Design: Michael Shevlin
Production Editor: Maude Spekes
Desktop Publishing Manager: Michael Shevlin
Managing Editor: Brent Gallenberger
Executive Editor: Del Franz
Executive Director, International Products and Programs:
Marilyn J. Rymniak

Special thanks to Amy Arner Sgarro, Enid Burns, Alison May, and
Pamela Vittorio

Manufactured in the United States of America
Published simultaneously in Canada

July 1998

10 9 8 7 6 5 4 3 2 1

Library of Congress Cataloging in Publication Data in progress

ISBN 0-684-85399-X

Table of Contents

How to Use This Book.........................vii

Chapter 1: Administration 1

Chapter 2: Bankruptcy 5

Chapter 3: Contracts I...........................9

Chapter 4: Contracts II 13

Chapter 5: Copyright I..........................17

Chapter 6: Copyright II.........................21

Chapter 7: Credit...............................25

Chapter 8: Crime I..............................29

Chapter 9: Crime II.............................33

Chapter 10: Custody............................37

Chapter 11: Debt...............................41

Chapter 12: Divorce............................45

Chapter 13: Employment 49

Chapter 14: Estate 53

Chapter 15: Harassment 57

Chapter 16: Health 61

Chapter 17: Immigration I 65

Chapter 18: Immigration II......................69

Chapter 19: Investment.........................73

Chapter 20: Juveniles 77

Chapter 21: Landlords 81

Chapter 22: Patents 85

Chapter 23: Personal Injury 89

Chapter 24: Social Security 93

Chapter 25: Taxes. 97

Chapter 26: Trademarks 101

Chapter 27: Traffic. 105

Chapter 28: Warranties 109

Chapter 29: Wills. 113

Chapter 30: Workplace 117

Index. 121

How to Use This Book

If you've studied English, you know that after you've reached a certain level, you need to work on refining and improving your vocabulary. As you become more familiar with the English language, you want to be able to use and understand the same sophisticated, professional legal vocabulary as your American classmates or colleagues.

Success with Legal Words is an invaluable tool for student or professional nonnative speakers of English seeking to attend law school or to enter the legal profession in the United States. It uses a variety of methods to help you to incorporate 450 legal words and phrases into your vocabulary. Certain phrases vary in meaning according to the context in which they are used, and may appear in more than one chapter.

Each of the 30 chapters in this book focuses on words or phrases that are related to a particular theme, such as *Credit* or *Trademarks*. Each chapter offers three different types of exercises that encourage you to contextualize and actively use these words or phrases. The first exercise consists of two columns in which 15 words or phrases listed in the left-hand column are to be matched with the correct definitions in the right-hand column. You should try to see how many phrases and meanings you can match up without using your dictionary. If this proves difficult, move on to the passages on the second page of the chapter and try reading them aloud to yourself or with a partner. The two conversations and the short talk you will find here use the terms from the matching list in relevant, realistic contexts. Seeing these phrases in their proper context should enable you to go back to the first exercise and match any terms that you were not able to figure out with their meanings.

Success with Legal Words

On the third page of each chapter, there is a fill-in-the-blank exercise that tests your understanding of the 15 words and expressions covered in the chapter. In this exercise you will "recycle" your vocabulary by putting the phrases that you learned in the matching exercise and passages into sentences, contextualizing them further. This will aid you in retaining them as "learned" vocabulary. Be aware that these exercises occasionally ask you to provide the term in a different part of speech or tense than that which is used in the matching list. This encourages you to develop and reinforce a sense of how the term is actively used in everyday legal English.

After you have completed the fill-in-the-blank exercise, you should review your work and check your answers in the answer keys on the fourth and final page of each chapter. Then read the conversations and short talk one more time to check your comprehension again.

You may work through these chapters in sequence, or by topic of interest. You can also look up unfamiliar words and phrases in the index and do the exercises that center around them. Whichever method you choose, you will master commonly used legal terms relevant to your chosen field of interest.

Good luck and enjoy using this book!

1 Administration

Match each word or phrase to its meaning:

1.	body	to make sure something is obeyed
2.	agency	dependent on
3.	to review	to relate to
4.	to delegate	ability to act effectively
5.	authority	a group regarded as an entity
6.	to enforce	to make
7.	to pertain	punishment for an offense
8.	to object	to draw out
9.	subject	coercive measure
10.	to terminate	to pass authority to someone else
11.	to elicit	power to command and enforce laws
12.	to render	to say one does not accept something
13.	power	branch of government
14.	penalty	to bring something to an end
15.	sanction	to examine an action; to correct an error

Success with Legal Words

Can you figure out the meanings of the italicized words in the following passages?

Conversation One:

KAREN: I'm really angry that the Federal Trade Commission has rejected my request for a new radio station. Do they have the *authority* to deny me?

PETER: Not necessarily. You can request a hearing on your case from an administrative law judge.

Conversation Two:

PETER: My father's benefits from the Veteran's Agency will end next month, and he needs them. How much will you charge to represent me in court?

KAREN: In a case of administrative law, you are allowed to represent yourself if you wish in the hearing in which the judge will *render* a decision.

Short Talk:

Administrative law is a *body* of law that governs *agencies* created by Congress or state legislatures, such as the Social Security Administration. Congress *delegates* the authority these agencies hold to them. Administrative agencies have the *power* to administer the law by creating and *enforcing* regulations. Most regulations *pertain* to providing some type of *penalty*, *sanction*, or benefit. Frequently, a user of the system, for example, a veteran, *objects* to the agency's decision to *terminate* a benefit, and seeks to have the benefit *reviewed* by an administrative law judge in a hearing. The judge meets with representatives from the agency and from the person seeking benefits. Each side presents its evidence, and may *elicit* testimony from witnesses. The judge *renders* a decision which is *subject* to review by a higher level within the agency or by a court.

Administration

Fill in the blanks to complete the sentences:

16. If a business receives a _____ for its practices and feels coerced into changing them, it can appeal under administrative law.

17. People who feel wronged by the action of an agency can request a _____ of their case.

18. The administrative judge has the authority to _____ a decision.

19. Many requests for review _____ to changes in benefits.

20. People often request a hearing when an agency decides _____ benefits.

21. Congress _____ federal authority to the agencies.

22. Federal agencies _____ a wide variety of rules and regulations under administrative law.

23. Most federal agencies are _____ working under administrative law.

24. Agencies can levy costly _____ to businesses that do not follow regulations.

25. When people or businesses _____ to a rule or regulation, they can request a review.

26. _____ charged with making and enforcing rules and regulations are governed by administrative law.

27. The judge's decision is _____ to review by a higher level of the agency or by a court.

28. Both sides will _____ testimony from witnesses.

29. Agencies have the _____ to regulate many aspects of people's lives.

30. Congress gives agencies the _____ to regulate many aspects of business.

Success with Legal Words

Answer Key

1. a group regarded as an entity
2. branch of government
3. to examine an action; to correct an error
4. to pass authority to someone else
5. power to command and enforce laws
6. to make sure something is obeyed
7. to relate to
8. to say you do not accept something
9. dependent on
10. to bring something to an end
11. to draw out
12. to make
13. ability to act effectively
14. punishment for an offense
15. coercive measure
16. sanction
17. review
18. render
19. pertain
20. to terminate
21. delegates
22. enforce
23. bodies
24. penalties
25. object
26. agencies
27. subject
28. elicit
29. authority
30. power

2 Bankruptcy

Match each word or phrase to its meaning:

1.	procedure	to suggest something be done
2.	obligations	to fulfill, release
3.	rare	clear; free of debt or obligations
4.	to file	acting for someone
5.	trustee	responsible for
6.	to exhaust	duty to do something
7.	to propose	drastic
8.	to repay	to engage in
9.	liable	person in charge of money or property
10.	to discharge	steps taken to bring an action to court
11.	extreme	the least favorable option
12.	clean slate	to pay money back
13.	last resort	unusual
14.	to pursue	to use up
15.	(on someone's) behalf	to make an official request

Success with Legal Words

Can you figure out the meanings of the italicized words in the following passages?

Conversation One:

DOUG: I'm drowning in debt; even the IRS is after me.

DOREEN: Filing for bankruptcy may be your best bet, but make sure you have *exhausted* all your other options.

Conversation Two:

DOUG: Shall I transfer my property to my wife, so it will be protected from the bankruptcy hearings?

DOREEN: I'm sorry to say that won't help. The *trustee* assigned to this case will discover the transfer and cancel it.

Short Talk:

Bankruptcy is a legal *procedure* that protects both individuals and businesses that cannot meet their financial *obligations* and their creditors. To begin the process, you must *file* papers on *behalf* of your client. (Only very rarely would a client choose to represent himself in a bankruptcy process.) The federal bankruptcy law is divided into chapters. Chapter 7 takes away most of the borrower's property. The court appoints a *trustee* to sell off the assets and distribute them to the creditors. Under Chapter 13, the borrower *proposes* a plan to *repay* the debt or a portion of the debt in installments from income. Chapter 11, used only by corporations, keeps creditors at bay while the business reorganizes itself to be more profitable. At the end of the bankruptcy process, the borrower is no longer *liable* for his or her debts. The court *discharges* the borrower's debts and the borrower then has a *clean* financial *slate*. The record of bankruptcy stays on his or her credit report for up to 10 years. Bankruptcy should be *pursued* only in *extreme* situations, after all other options are *exhausted*. It should be used only as a *last resort* because of its long-lasting consequences.

Bankruptcy

Fill in the blanks to complete the sentences:

16. After bankruptcy is complete, the borrower is no longer _____ for the debt.
17. To start the process, an attorney files for bankruptcy on _____ of the client.
18. Bankruptcy should be _____ only after all other options have been exhausted.
19. It is _____ that a person would represent himself against a creditor.
20. Bankruptcy should be considered only after _____ all other reasonable options.
21. Under Chapter 13, the borrower _____ his or her debt over an extended period of time.
22. Bankruptcy _____ the borrower from his or her debts.
23. Bankruptcy clears a person or business of all financial _____.
24. Bankruptcy should be used only in _____ situations.
25. Under Chapter 13, the borrower _____ a plan to honor his debts over time.
26. It is in your interests to maintain a _____ financial _____ if you can.
27. Bankruptcy paperwork is _____ with a special federal court.
28. Because bankruptcy stays on the credit record for at least 10 years, use it only as a _____.
29. Bankruptcy _____ are almost always handled by an attorney.
30. The court will appoint a _____ to supervise the process.

Success with Legal Words

Answer Key

1. steps taken to bring an action to court
2. duty to do something
3. unusual
4. to make an official request
5. person in charge of money or property
6. to use up
7. to suggest something be done
8. to pay money back
9. responsible for
10. to fulfill, release
11. drastic
12. clear; free of debt or obligations
13. the least favorable option
14. to engage in
15. acting for someone
16. liable
17. behalf
18. pursued
19. rare
20. exhausting
21. repays
22. discharges
23. obligations
24. extreme
25. proposes
26. clean (financial) slate
27. filed
28. last resort
29. procedures
30. trustee

3 Contracts I

Match each word or phrase to its meaning:

1. agreement — to enforce
2. competent — comprehension of the meaning of something
3. party — division within a classification
4. offer — an understanding between two parties
5. understanding — openly stated
6. to compel — to separate into parts
7. to bind — person or company involved
8. to perform — suggested by logical necessity
9. to divide — adequately qualified, of good mental capacity
10. category — fair treatment
11. express — to state or declare
12. implied — to acknowledge openly
13. to utter — to do something to completion
14. justice — proposal to do something
15. to avow — to obligate someone

Success with Legal Words

Can you figure out the meanings of the italicized words in the following passages?

Conversation One:

JAN: This part of the contract makes me nervous, and I don't want to sign it.

ENID: You can reject the entire contract, or just cross out the part you wish to delete.

JAN: I'll make sure my changes end up on all the copies of the *agreement*.

Conversation Two:

JAN: This contract isn't what you had discussed with me.

ENID: How can that be? The other *party* said he would make the changes I asked for.

JAN: Did you read the contract before signing it? Or did you just assume that the corrections had been made?

Short Talk:

Contracts are *agreements* between two or more *competent parties*. In a contract, an *offer* is made and accepted, and each party benefits. Contracts can be written or oral, formal or informal, or simply *understood* by the two parties. To *compel* some contracts, one must put them in writing. A contract typically creates an obligation to do or avoid doing something, or to pay a sum of money. Contracts are a wide-ranging area of the law, as they cover every instance in which one party becomes *bound* to another to *perform* an obligation or to pay money. Contracts are *divided* into *express* contracts, in which the terms of the agreement are openly *uttered* and avowed at the time the parties make the contract, and *implied* contracts, which are dictated by reason, *justice*, and that which the law presumes should be *performed*.

Contracts I

Fill in the blanks to complete the sentences:

16. A contract _____ together the signing parties.
17. All parties signing the contract must be _____ and understand its obligations.
18. In an express contract, the parties _____ the agreement by making the contract.
19. Implied contracts assume _____ in the compact, such as that a worker will be paid a commensurate wage.
20. Contracts can be valid even if they are simply an _____ between the parties.
21. Contracts often indicate a service that a party will _____.
22. _____ contracts concern conditions clearly stated in the contract.
23. It is easier _____ a contract if it is in writing.
24. Lady Fortescue claimed that the terms of the express contract had never been _____, and that she was under no obligation to honor it.
25. There are two _____ of contracts: express and implied.
26. We should consult the other _____ before we finalize this contract; they might not like our latest additions.
27. A contract is an _____ to do something or pay some amount.
28. In a contract, one party makes an _____ to another.
29. Contracts are _____ into different categories.
30. _____ contracts are those in which a reasonable assumption is made that something will happen.

Success with Legal Words

Answer Key

1. an understanding between two parties
2. adequately qualified, of good mental capacity
3. person or company involved
4. proposal to do something
5. comprehension of the meaning of something
6. to enforce
7. to obligate someone
8. to do something to completion
9. to separate into parts
10. division within a classification
11. openly stated
12. suggested by logical necessity
13. to state or declare
14. fair treatment
15. to acknowledge openly
16. binds
17. competent
18. avow
19. justice
20. understanding
21. perform
22. express
23. to compel
24. uttered
25. categories
26. party
27. agreement
28. offer
29. divided
30. implied

4 Contracts II

Match each word or phrase to its meaning:

1.	voluntary	interchangeable
2.	to omit	to act formally, making something effective
3.	sufficient	directed and received in equal amount
4.	reciprocal	to take for granted
5.	mutual	incentive
6.	assent	to leave out
7.	to withhold	to take upon oneself
8.	motive	a fair price for goods or services
9.	solemnity	to refrain from giving
10.	to deliver	material value
11.	to assume	arising from one's own free will
12.	to undertake	thing that has been done
13.	worth	agreement
14.	value	as much as is needed
15.	action	in deep earnestness

Success with Legal Words

Can you figure out the meanings of the italicized words in the following passages?

Conversation One:

MIKE: My landlord says he won't *undertake* to fix my unsafe back steps. He says our lease doesn't require him to do this.

CHRIS: Keeping the unit safe is an implied contract of a rental agreement. If he refuses to fix them, you can *withhold* rent, or take *action* against him.

Conversation Two:

CHRIS: This contract confuses me. It doesn't seem to say exactly what the other party is going to do for me. I need to make sure she pays me within 30 days.

MIKE: Contracts are *reciprocal*. What does she need you to do for her?

CHRIS: I *assume* that I need to prove the *worth* of the jewelry I sold her. She's questioning its true *value*.

MIKE: Sounds like that may be why she hasn't paid you yet.

Short Talk:

Express contracts are divided into three types: parol, under seal, and of record. A parol contract is a *voluntary* agreement made orally or in writing upon consideration between two or more parties to do a lawful act or to *omit* to do something. To constitute a *sufficient* parol agreement, there must be reciprocal or *mutual assent* among those entering the contract. All parties must have a good *motive* for making the contract. Under seal contracts include deeds or bonds. These are not merely written; they are *delivered* by the bound parties, giving them a higher degree of *solemnity*. The highest express contract is that of record, such as judgments and bail.

Contracts II

Fill in the blanks to complete the sentences:

16. A number of factors must be in place to constitute a _____ agreement.

17. A contract under seal, such as a deed, has a _____ befitting its higher rank over a simple contract.

18. If either party _____ its agreement to a term, the contract is incomplete.

19. Implied contracts presume that reasonable _____ will take place between the parties, even without them being expressed.

20. All parties covered under the contract must give their _____.

21. If you take goods from a merchant, an implied contract assumes you will pay her the _____ of the goods.

22. Each party must enter the contract with good _____.

23. A contract made under seal is usually _____ by the party bound.

24. Implied contracts _____ certain actions should take place, even if these actions are not expressed.

25. Implied contracts presume that persons in the contract will _____ to perform certain actions.

26. Contracts can declare that one of the parties will _____ to do something.

27. There must be _____ assent between the parties for the contract to be valid.

28. Assuming that you will pay a laborer his or her true _____ is an example of an implied contract.

29. All parties must enter a contract _____.

30. A contract should serve the _____ needs of the parties.

Success with Legal Words

Answer Key

1. arising from one's own free will
2. to leave out
3. as much as is needed
4. interchangeable
5. directed and received in equal amount
6. agreement
7. to refrain from giving
8. incentive
9. in deep earnestness
10. to act formally, making something effective
11. to take for granted
12. to take upon oneself
13. material value
14. a fair price for goods or services
15. thing that has been done
16. sufficient
17. solemnity
18. withholds
19. actions
20. assent
21. value
22. motives
23. delivered
24. assume
25. undertake
26. omit
27. reciprocal
28. worth
29. voluntarily
30. mutual

5 Copyright I

Match each word or phrase to its meaning:

1.	to exist	to have as a visible characteristic
2.	to fix	something that is true and real
3.	tangible	mindful of something
4.	media	to suppose that something is correct
5.	to bear	to negotiate something
6.	formal	to claim
7.	to establish	positional advantage
8.	to presume	substance from which an item is made
9.	fact	to be
10.	to infringe	types of artistic techniques, based on materials
11.	leverage	observable and appraisable
12.	to bargain	to break a law or right
13.	to contend	to place securely
14.	aware	clearly and legally written
15.	material	to introduce as an entity

Success with Legal Words

Can you identify the meanings of the italicized words in the following passages?

Conversation One:

BEN: Are you *aware* that your copyright application won't go through? You cannot *formally* copyright an idea.

PAULA: How do people copyright books, then?

BEN: In that instance they are copyrighting the expression of an idea in a work, which is subject to copyright.

Conversation Two:

RALPH: Did you manage to stop that man from *infringing* on your toy copyright?

PHOEBE: Yes, although he *contends* that he wasn't *aware* that my work was copyrighted.

Short Talk:

Copyright allows original, created works to be protected to prevent others from copying them without the creator's permission and without paying the creator a fee. A copyright enters into *existence* upon being *fixed* in a *tangible medium* of expression, whether or not the creator of the work registers it and the work *bears* a copyright notice. Or, put more simply, as soon as someone creates a work that can be copyrighted, it is automatically copyrighted. However, the *formal* registration and notice process is recommended. Registering a copyright within five years of the date of first publication *establishes* the *presumption* of the *facts* on the registration certificate. By registering copyright prior to an *infringement*, the copyright holder preserves certain legal rights, which give him or her ethical and financial *leverage* in *bargaining* to settle infringement disputes. The same rules of copyright apply when the *material* exists on the Internet.

Copyright I

Fill in the blanks to complete the sentences:

16. Encourage your clients to enter their work under the _____ copyright registration system.
17. Copyright is present if the creator _____ it in the work.
18. Copyright protects a variety of creative _____, like books, films, software, artwork, and music.
19. The Copyright Office registration form will ask for _____ about the creator, as well as one or two copies of the work.
20. When a work bears a copyright notice, no one can say he was not _____ that copyright existed.
21. Registering the work within five years of its first publication means that the Copyright Office will _____ that the information on the certificate is true.
22. Copyright registration prevents others from _____ upon work.
23. Sometimes, stating your legal rights as the registered holder of a copyright is enough to let you _____ with infringers.
24. A work has copyright protection whether or not it _____ a notice of copyright.
25. As long as it expresses an idea, any type of _____ is subject to copyright, no matter what medium it is created in.
26. Simply having a copyright registration before there is an infringement gives the person with the copyright significant _____ over an infringer.
27. Registering the work with the Copyright Office _____ it as the property of the creator.
28. Registering a copyright can deter those who would _____ they didn't know the work was subject to protection.
29. Copyright _____ as soon as a work that is subject to copyright is created.
30. If the work of expression is _____ and can be discerned, it is likely that copyright will exist.

Success with Legal Words

Answer Key

1. to be
2. to introduce as an entity
3. observable and appraisable
4. types of artistic techniques, based on materials
5. to have as a visible characteristic
6. clearly and legally written
7. to place securely
8. to suppose something is correct
9. something that is true and real
10. to break a law or right
11. positional advantage
12. to negotiate something
13. to claim
14. mindful of something
15. substance from which an item is made
16. formal
17. fixes
18. media
19. facts
20. aware
21. presume
22. infringing
23. bargain
24. bears
25. material
26. leverage
27. establishes
28. contend
29. exists
30. tangible

6 Copyright II

Match each word or phrase to its meaning:

1.	to restore	to suggest what should be done
2.	public domain	to say clearly
3.	to fail	to form
4.	to renew	to ascertain by definitive characteristics
5.	to advise	to bring back to a previous condition
6.	to identify	something that contributes to something
7.	hierarchy	difficult
8.	to constitute	something singled out
9.	contract	to neglect
10.	complex	to deem to be, to take into account
11.	to state	to transfer rights or interests
12.	select	works no longer under copyright
13.	to assign	classification according to rank
14.	factor	to grant again so that it continues for a further period
15.	to consider	legal agreement between two or more parties

Success with Legal Words

Can you figure out the meanings of the italicized words in the following passages?

Conversation One:

BRENT: I neglected to *renew* the copyright on my song. Now I've lost it to the public domain.

LISA: Don't worry—the laws changed recently. Your work is still protected.

Conversation Two:

LISA: I was working on a contract to develop this program, so I think I own it and can copyright it.

BRENT: That's a *complex* problem. It might belong to your employer. Did your contract discuss work for hire?

Short Talk:

Recent legislation has *restored* copyright protection to works of foreign origin that had entered the *public domain*. In the past, *failure* to renew copyright in works caused the works to fall into the public domain. That no longer happens, but it is still *advisable* to *renew* copyright with the Copyright Office. This involves completing a form, returning the form with the required fee, sending two copies of the work, and some *identifying* material, if requested. For published works, submit the best edition of the work. A well-defined *hierarchy* exists as to what *constitutes* the best edition. Work for hire results from either an employment relationship or a *contract* to create a work. Determining whether an employment situation exists is *complex* because many *factors* must be *considered* to make that determination. Without an employment relationship, a work may be a work for hire only if it is one of a *select* type, the contract clearly *states* it was a work for hire, and both parties sign the contract prior to work beginning. Copyright can also be *assigned* from one party to another.

Copyright II

Fill in the blanks to complete the sentences:

16. Under new laws, even when the creator does not _____ the copyright, the material is still protected.
17. You can _____ copyright to someone else as long as there is a signed agreement.
18. Contracts should clearly _____ who owns the work.
19. Work for hire is difficult to judge because so many different _____ go into writing the contract.
20. The Copyright Office may ask your client to submit _____ material related to the work being registered.
21. Works in the _____ do not receive copyright protection.
22. Ask the Copyright Office to help you determine what _____ a best edition if you are unsure.
23. There is an established _____ to determine which edition of a work is considered the best edition.
24. The work considered work for hire must be of the _____ type described in the work for hire contract.
25. Work created under a _____ between an employer and a freelance employee can be difficult to copyright.
26. It is still best to _____ your clients to register their works.
27. Recent legislation has _____ ownership of works that were in the public domain to their foreign owners.
28. If a creator _____ that there are similarities between his work and later work, he may claim copyright infringement.
29. People who _____ to renew their copyright found their work in the public domain.
30. Understanding who owns original work is a _____ undertaking unless ownership is clearly stated in the signed contract.

Success with Legal Words

Answer Key

1. to bring back to a previous condition
2. works no longer under copyright
3. to neglect
4. to grant again so that it continues for a further period
5. to suggest what should be done
6. to ascertain by definitive characteristics
7. classification according to rank
8. to form
9. legal agreement between two or more parties
10. difficult
11. to say clearly
12. something singled out
13. to transfer rights or interest
14. something that contributes to something
15. to deem to be, to take into account
16. renew
17. assign
18. state
19. factors
20. identifying
21. public domain
22. constitutes
23. hierarchy
24. select
25. contract
26. advise
27. restored
28. considers
29. failed
30. complex

7 Credit

Match each word or phrase to its meaning:

1. access
2. convenient
3. minor
4. hazardous
5. punctual
6. credit history
7. to divulge
8. to order
9. to evaluate
10. to deny
11. provision
12. installment
13. to regulate
14. to disseminate
15. to grant

on time
to command or direct
personal record of payment of bills
allowance made for something
favorable to one's needs
to control according to a rule
to declare to be untrue
trivial
to allow to have
to make known
to spread widely
means of approaching
successive payment in settlement of a debt
dangerous
to ascertain the worth of something

Success with Legal Words

Can you figure out the meanings of the italicized words in the following passages?

Conversation One:

TREVOR: I applied for a credit card, but was *denied.*

MAUREEN: The credit company is obligated to tell you why.

Conversation Two:

MAUREEN: What kinds of questions can loan officers ask me?

TREVOR: Only ones that relate to whether you can repay the loan. You don't have to *divulge* anything else.

Short Talk:

Having *access* to credit is important and *convenient.* Important because without credit, it is almost impossible to buy a house or a car. And convenient because many *minor* transactions, like buying a plane ticket, are based on using a credit card. Credit can be *hazardous* to financial health because it makes it possible to spend more than you earn. People who do not pay their debts *punctually* risk paying late fees, penalties, and higher rates of interest, plus damaging their credit records. Federal laws *protect* applicants from discrimination by requiring that each applicant be evaluated only on their credit-worthiness. Special *provisions* are made for women to build *credit histories* in their own names. Credit companies must also make certain an applicant is fully informed before he or she signs a credit *installment* agreement. While the government *regulates* the credit industry, they still have amazing power to collect and *disseminate* information. Credit bureaus collect information on how much money people owe and whether or not they pay their bills on time. Credit bureaus sell this information to other creditors, employers, and insurers. When someone applies for credit, the creditor *orders* a copy of the record and reviews it as part of its credit-*granting* process.

Credit

Fill in the blanks to complete the sentences:

16. Most people have _____ to at least one form of credit.
17. Credit cards make small purchases _____.
18. Sometimes, even _____ purchases can only be made with a credit card.
19. Credit is easy to get, which can make it _____ to your financial health.
20. Paying the minimum due and paying it _____ is crucial.
21. You can build up a good _____ by paying all your credit card bills on time.
22. If you have been denied credit, the company must promptly _____ why.
23. When you apply for credit and sometimes for a job, the creditor will _____ a copy of your credit history.
24. Creditors can _____ applicants based only on credit worthiness, and not any other factors.
25. When creditors _____ a credit application, they must give a reason why.
26. To help women build credit in their own names, special _____ for this are guaranteed under law.
27. The law makes it necessary that applicants clearly understand what they are signing when they sign a credit _____ agreement.
28. The federal government _____ the activities of the credit industry.
29. Credit bureaus first collect, then _____ information about individual accounts.
30. Creditors try to _____ credit only to those who can repay the loans they receive.

Success with Legal Words

Answer Key

1. means of approaching
2. favorable to one's needs
3. trivial
4. dangerous
5. on time
6. personal record of payment of bills
7. to make known
8. to command or direct
9. to ascertain the worth of something
10. to declare to be untrue
11. allowance made for something
12. successive payment in settlement of a debt
13. to control according to a rule
14. to spread widely
15. to allow to have
16. access
17. convenient
18. minor
19. hazardous
20. punctually
21. credit history
22. divulge
23. order
24. evaluate
25. deny
26. provisions
27. installment
28. regulates
29. disseminate
30. grant

8 Crime I

Match each word or phrase to its meaning:

1.	act	to evaluate
2.	to group	statement that one thinks something wrong has been done to one
3.	to prescribe	required
4.	classification	to reveal
5.	case	possible crime and its investigation
6.	misdemeanor	reasonable grounds to believe someone is guilty
7.	complaint	official document that allows someone to do something
8.	to demonstrate	something that is done
9.	to assess	ability
10.	to decide	grouping by categories
11.	warrant	apart in space or time
12.	necessary	less serious crime
13.	probable cause	to place or arrange into a unit
14.	distance	to conclude
15.	capacity	to guide, to set down as a rule

Success with Legal Words

Can you figure out the meanings of the italicized words in the following passages?

Conversation One:

MR. BAINES: Officer, you don't have a *warrant* for my client's arrest.

OFFICER KELLY: We needed to make an arrest on the spot. The wait for the warrant would have meant losing the accused in this *case.*

Conversation Two:

MR. BAINES: Why did you feel the urgency to arrest my client without a warrant?

OFFICER KELLY: We had *probable cause.* There was a report of a burglary a few blocks away, and we saw your client carrying a television that matched the description of one taken from the crime site.

Short Talk:

A crime is an *act* against the law, generally committed with an intent to willfully and knowingly do something that is wrong. Crimes are *grouped* into two *classifications: misdemeanors* and felonies. Misdemeanors are less serious crimes for which the law *prescribes* punishment in the form of a fine, or a short prison term, or both. If the accused person lacks the mental *capacity* to form a criminal intent, he or she cannot be held responsible for the action. A felony or criminal prosecution begins with a *complaint* or information that *demonstrates* the charge. A judge *assesses* the information to *decide* if the accused should be arrested. A *warrant* is *necessary* to make an arrest. However, the police can make an arrest without a warrant when there is *probable cause* to believe a person committed the crime, such as if he is found near the crime scene. A warrant is needed to arrest someone at a *distance* from the crime scene.

Crime I

Fill in the blanks to complete the sentences:

16. A judge _____ if there is enough suspicion to issue an arrest or search warrant.
17. With misdemeanors, the law _____ the sentence.
18. The legal system is full of criminal _____.
19. Warrants are _____ to make most arrests and to search property.
20. You can be arrested without a warrant if the police believe that they have _____.
21. An arrest starts with a _____ of a crime.
22. To get an arrest warrant, the police must _____ reason to believe a suspect is likely to be guilty.
23. Criminals try to put as much _____ as possible between themselves and the crime scene.
24. A judge will _____ the information available before issuing a warrant.
25. A misdemeanor is a less serious _____ of crime than a felony.
26. A crime is an _____ that breaks the law.
27. When a _____ is issued for arrest, the judge has decided there is sufficient reason to detain someone.
28. Because her crime was classifed as a _____, she got off with a fine.
29. Crimes are _____ into different categories according to their severity.
30. If a person does not have the mental _____ to know the act was a crime, he or she is not considered legally responsible for it.

Success with Legal Words

Answer Key

1. something that is done
2. to place or arrange in a unit
3. to guide, to set down as a rule
4. grouping by categories
5. possible crime and its investigation
6. less serious crime
7. statement that one thinks something wrong has been done to one
8. to reveal
9. to evaluate
10. to conclude
11. official document that allows someone to do something
12. required
13. reasonable grounds to believe that someone is guilty
14. apart in space or time
15. ability
16. decides
17. prescribes
18. cases
19. necessary
20. probable cause
21. complaint
22. demonstrate
23. distance
24. assess
25. classification
26. act
27. warrant
28. misdemeanor
29. grouped
30. capacity

9 Crime II

Match each word or phrase to its meaning:

1. custody — to stay
2. to warn — to wait to participate in
3. to question — existence at hand
4. to remain — quick
5. presence — to find guilty
6. to arraign — immediate charge and control
7. plea — to deny
8. speedy — to conclude
9. to cross-examine — to subject to detailed questioning in court
10. to refute — to discuss at length a matter of importance
11. to prove — to give notice beforehand of danger
12. to deliberate — to give a summation or conclusion
13. to convict — to call a defendant before a court to answer charges
14. to sum up — accused's answer to a charge
15. to stand — to establish the truth or validity

Success with Legal Words

Can you figure out the meanings of the italicized words in the following passages?

Conversation One:

MR. BAINES: Have you *warned* my client of his rights?

OFFICER KELLY: We told him he had the right to the *presence* of his attorney.

Conversation Two:

MR. TUCCI: Don't believe my business partner. It was he, not I, who was stealing from customers.

MS. MITCHELL: You will have the chance *to prove* your side of the story when I *cross-examine* him.

Short Talk:

Any person taken into *custody* has rights. He must be *warned* before any questioning begins that he has the right to *remain* silent, that any statement made can be used against him, that he has the right to the *presence* of an attorney, and if he cannot afford a lawyer, one will be provided one by the state. After an arrest, the person accused of the crime is given a hearing before a judge to determine whether or not an offense was committed and whether or not there is probable cause to believe the arrested person committed the crime. If the accused is *arraigned*, he or she will *stand* trial and enter a *plea*. A *speedy* trial is guaranteed by the U.S. Constitution. In this trial, the accused may present evidence to *refute* the prosecution's case and to prove his innocence. He can also *cross-examine* the prosecution's witnesses. Once all the evidence is submitted and the prosecuting and defense attorneys have made final statements to the jury to *sum up* their cases, the jury *deliberates* and gives its verdict. If the jury's verdict is guilty, the defendant is *convicted* and the court will sentence him. If the jury delivers a not guilty verdict, the accused can go free.

Crime II

Fill in the blanks to complete the sentences:

16. If the jury votes to _____ the accused, he or she is found guilty.
17. Persons in custody have the right to an attorney during any police _____.
18. Each side has the right to _____ witnesses to elicit vital information.
19. The accused will enter a _____ of innocence or guilt before a judge.
20. At the end of the trial, the attorneys for each side will _____ their arguments.
21. The goal of a trial is _____ the guilt or innocence of the accused.
22. Among the accused's civil rights is the right to be _____ that he or she can remain silent.
23. You have the right to _____ silent to protect yourself.
24. In a criminal case, the accused must enter a plea if he or she is _____.
25. The right to a _____ trial is guaranteed by the Constitution.
26. The jury will _____ to make a consensus decision on guilt or innocence.
27. If the accused pleads not guilty, he will then _____ trial.
28. Once the police take someone into _____, that person has specific rights that must be honored.
29. The state will pay for the _____ of an attorney for those who cannot pay.
30. Both sides can call witnesses _____ claims made by the other side.

Success with Legal Words

Answer Key

1. immediate charge and control
2. to give notice beforehand of danger
3. to establish the truth or validity
4. to stay
5. existence at hand
6. to call a defendant before a court to answer charges
7. accused's answer to a charge
8. quick
9. to subject to detailed questioning in court
10. to deny
11. to conclude
12. to discuss at length a matter of importance
13. to find guilty
14. to give a summation or conclusion
15. to wait to participate in
16. convict
17. questioning
18. cross-examine
19. plea
20. sum up
21. to prove
22. warned
23. remain
24. arraigned
25. speedy
26. deliberate
27. stand
28. custody
29. presence
30. to refute

10 Custody

Match each word or phrase to its meaning:

1. custom — to give preference to
2. joint — to formally request
3. to award — firmly established
4. reluctant — to perceive the difference in
5. suitable — to stimulate
6. foster care — to put into practice
7. to favor — long-established practice
8. stable — shorter, condensed version of something
9. priority — general concept
10. to motivate — to give
11. notion — protective care
12. to petition — unwilling
13. to exercise — shared
14. outline — superior importance
15. to distinguish — qualified

Success with Legal Words

Can you figure out the meanings of the italicized words in the following passages?

Conversation One:

ANDY: My ex-wife won't let me *exercise* my visitation rights.

SYLVIA: You can *petition* the court to force her to let you see your children.

Conversation Two:

CURTIS: My wife and I are divorcing. Aren't courts *reluctant* to give custody of small children to the father?

SYLVIA: That's the *custom*, but it isn't the law. Courts are supposed to ignore the sex of the parents.

Short Talk:

One can *distinguish* between physical custody, which refers to the responsibility of taking care of a child, and legal custody, which means decision making for the interests of the child. *Joint* custody means that at least some aspects of custody are shared between the parents. States are often willing *to award* joint legal custody, but are more *reluctant* to award joint physical custody unless the parents can cooperate with each other. In cases where neither parent can *suitably* assume custody of the children, the court may seek a *foster care* arrangement. The court *favors* the parent who can best maintain *stability* in the child's surroundings. Courts are supposed to give the best interests of the child the highest *priority*, but judges are often *motivated* by their own *notions* of best interests. To avoid conflict, many courts prefer to work out a parenting agreement that sets the visitation schedule and *outlines* responsibilities. The U.S. Supreme Court has ruled it unconstitutional to consider race when a noncustodial parent *petitions* for a change in custody, and a few states bar taking a parent's sexual orientation into consideration in such cases.

Custody

Fill in the blanks to complete the sentences:

16. If the parents cannot take responsibility for their children, the court will appoint a _____ provider.
17. A noncustodial parent will almost always _____ some right to visitation.
18. Judges can be _____ by their own biases as to what is in the child's best interest.
19. A noncustodial parent can _____ for a change in custody.
20. The best interests of the child is the court's highest _____.
21. The primary goal of the custody arrangement is to create the most _____ arrangement for the child.
22. The court is supposed _____ the parent who can best care for the child.
23. Courts can _____ sole or joint custody.
24. The court looks to keep the child's life as _____ as possible through maintaining school and community ties.
25. Many courts are _____ to assign joint physical custody unless the parents can prove they can make it work.
26. Courts can award _____ custody, in which the parents concerned share in the decision making and the care of the child.
27. Judges can make decisions based on their _____ of the best interests of the child.
28. It is only a _____ that the mother tends to get custody of the children.
29. Some courts _____ the specifics of a joint custody agreement.
30. Some states _____ between legal and physical custody.

Success with Legal Words

Answer Key

1. long-established practice
2. shared
3. to give
4. unwilling
5. qualified
6. protective care
7. to give preference to
8. firmly established
9. superior importance
10. to stimulate
11. general concept
12. to formally request
13. to put into practice
14. shorter, condensed version of something
15. to perceive the difference in
16. foster care
17. exercise
18. motivated
19. petition
20. priority
21. suitable
22. to favor
23. award
24. stable
25. reluctant
26. joint
27. notion
28. custom
29. outline
30. distinguish

11 Debt

Match each word or phrase to its meaning:

1. creditor — to start legal proceedings
2. to impose — to restore harmony
3. standard — to find a solution
4. to restrict — to set boundaries
5. to resolve — profits
6. dispute — to withhold for debt owed
7. to settle — person who is owed money
8. to sue — money owed for goods or services
9. to garnish — to keep within limits
10. to recover — to take possession
11. to limit — disagreement
12. to seize — a degree of conduct
13. property — to get back that which has been lost
14. proceeds — to establish as compulsory
15. debt — items owned

Success with Legal Words

Can you figure out the meanings of the italicized words in the following passages?

Conversation One:

FRANK: We are over our heads in *debt* and getting nasty phone calls from debt collectors.

ABBY: Don't avoid them. It will only hurt you in the long run. Try to work out a favorable plan, such as a smaller monthly payment over a longer period of time.

Conversation Two:

FRANK: The collection agency has written to say they are taking action. They will probably *garnish* my wages to retrieve what I owe them or *seize* my property.

ABBY: That's terrible. Is that legal?

Short Talk:

If a client has trouble paying bills, encourage him to contact his *creditors* immediately. Sometimes, smaller monthly payments are a possibility for a while. The Fair Debt Collection Practices Act *imposes* a *standard* on the activities of debt collectors and gives people rights in dealing with them. The law *restricts* when and where debt collectors can call, methods of collection, and methods of *resolving disputes* regarding the amounts of debt owed. If the matter is not *settled*, a debt collection agency can *sue* you or *garnish* your wages to *recover* the money. Federal law *limits* how much creditors can garnish from a paycheck. Under certain conditions that vary state to state, a debt collector can *seize property*. If a creditor seizes some property and auctions it off, the *proceeds* go to paying the debt. Any extra is kept by the individual. If there is a dispute over how much is owed, the individual must write to the collection agent within 30 days of being contacted.

Debt

Fill in the blanks to complete the sentences:

16. Try to work out a favorable plan with the _____ to whom your client owes money.
17. The law has _____ guidelines that debt collectors must follow.
18. While debt collectors can work to recover what they are owed, there are _____ they must follow.
19. The law _____ the times and places a creditor can call about a debt.
20. Work to _____ the problem to both parties' mutual advantage.
21. If your client _____ the amount of money owed, get that cleared up in writing.
22. Debt collectors eventually end up _____ the matter by serious means.
23. Your client can be _____ for what he owes.
24. Laws about _____ wages vary from state to state.
25. Garnishing wages is one way creditors will attempt _____ a bad debt.
26. States have a _____ on how much per paycheck can be garnished.
27. Some creditors will attempt _____ property to recover what they are owed.
28. Every state exempts some kind of personal _____ from seizure and sale.
29. If property is sold, the _____ go to paying the debt.
30. The amount of _____ held collectively in the United States is staggering.

Success with Legal Words

Answer Key

1. person who is owed money
2. to establish as compulsory
3. a degree of conduct
4. to keep within limits
5. to find a solution
6. disagreement
7. to restore harmony
8. to start legal proceedings
9. to withhold for debt owed
10. to get back that which has been lost
11. to set boundaries
12. to take possession
13. items owned
14. profits
15. money owed for goods or services
16. creditors
17. imposed
18. standards
19. restricts
20. resolve
21. disputes
22. settling
23. sued
24. garnishing
25. to recover
26. limit
27. to seize
28. property
29. proceeds
30. debt

12 Divorce

Match each word or phrase to its meaning:

1. to swear — to start again
2. grounds — conditions or facts
3. to serve — to convince
4. to answer — basic reasons
5. to issue — opposing
6. decree — impossible to resolve
7. circumstances — to give out
8. irreconcilable — the common good of the people
9. jurisdiction — order from the court
10. to reconcile — to make an oath that something is true
11. to resume — to respond to
12. to satisfy — legal power over an area
13. contrary — to give someone an official writ
14. public interest — to bring back together
15. to cohabitate — to live together

Success with Legal Words

Can you figure out the meanings of the italicized words in the following passages?

Conversation One:

ELTON: I want to go ahead with the divorce proceedings.

MELANIE: That shouldn't be any problem. You haven't *cohabited* for two years and have no desire to *resume* living together.

Conversation Two:

ELTON: We have *irreconcilable* differences in our relationship. That's generally enough to get a no-fault divorce.

MELANIE: Things were certainly different for my parents.

Short Talk:

An action for separation or divorce begins by filing a signed and *sworn* statement with the court indicating that sufficient *grounds* for relief from marriage exist. After the complaint is filed, it is *served* on the defendant. The defendant has time to respond and file an *answer* to the complaint. The family court can *issue* a *decree* for divorce under a number of *circumstances*. The court will grant a divorce when the marriage is irretrievably broken. A divorce will be granted when the parties have lived separate and apart under a decree of separation from any court of competent *jurisdiction*, the term of separation has expired, and no *reconciliation* has occurred. The couple can get a divorce when they have lived separate and apart for two years or more under a decree of separate maintenance, and have not reconciled. They can get a divorce when there is no reasonable likelihood that cohabitation will *resume* and the court is *satisfied* that it would not be harsh or oppressive or *contrary* to the *public interest* to grant the divorce on the grounds requested.

Divorce

Fill in the blanks to complete the sentences:

16. If it is doubtful they will ever again _____, many couples decide to get a divorce.

17. After they have been initiated, the court _____ the divorce papers to the defendant.

18. Legally, the court must be _____ that it would not be harsh or oppressive to grant a divorce.

19. The most common reason for divorce listed on the divorce decree is _____ differences.

20. Many divorce proceedings follow a separation decree from a court of a competent _____.

21. Under a separation decree, many couples see if they can _____ their differences.

22. Like most legal documents, the plaintiff must _____ that the statements contained in it are true.

23. Courts will grant a divorce if there is no reason to believe that a couple living apart will _____ living together.

24. A divorce is easily granted under a number of _____, including adultery.

25. The defendant has time to _____ to and correct any of the comments in the divorce.

26. The courts will want to assure that the divorce will not be _____ to the public interest.

27. Mrs. Smith argued that her husband's gambling away of all her savings was reasonable _____ for divorce.

28. In years past, ascertaining the impact of the divorce on the _____ at large was a concern.

29. Divorce _____ are finalized and issued by the family court system.

30. The court may refuse to _____ a divorce decree if it considers that the couple's reasons for breaking up are not valid.

Success with Legal Words

Answer Key

1. to make an oath that something is true
2. basic reasons
3. to give someone an official writ
4. to respond to
5. to give out
6. order from the court
7. conditions or facts
8. impossible to reconcile
9. legal power over an area
10. to bring back together
11. to start again
12. to convince
13. opposing
14. the common good of the people
15. to live together
16. cohabitate
17. serves
18. satisfied
19. irreconcilable
20. jurisdiction
21. reconcile
22. swear
23. resume
24. circumstances
25. answer
26. contrary
27. grounds
28. public interest
29. decrees
30. issue

13 Employment

Match each word or phrase to its meaning:

1.	to pass	the least possible
2.	to protect	to engage the services of
3.	right	to supply
4.	to hire	habit, routine
5.	minimum	rigid
6.	interview	to direct the course of something
7.	prospective	to approve or make into law
8.	practice	to make sure that something is correct
9.	qualification	conversation arranged to discuss a matter
10.	to conduct	to deal with
11.	to provide	legal entitlement
12.	strict	to act with prejudice against
13.	to check	expected
14.	to handle	to defend against harm
15.	to discriminate against	ability that suits a person to a task

Success with Legal Words

Can you figure out the meanings of the italicized words in the following passages?

Conversation One:

JULIA: We have job candidates coming today. I need to find out if they have the right *qualifications* for the position. What can I ask them?

ROY: You can only ask them questions that relate directly to the job they will do.

Conversation Two:

JULIA: I think I may have been *discriminated against* during my job *interview*. They asked me about my religion and my family.

ROY: Your *rights* have been violated. Our laws *protect* you from being asked personal questions in an interview.

Short Talk:

The federal government has *passed* many laws that *protect* the *rights* of workers in the workplace. These laws cover hiring *practices*, *minimum* wage, and work safety. During an *interview*, a *prospective* employer cannot ask questions about anything that does not relate to an applicant's *qualifications* for the job. Personal questions are limited to those that relate to a person's actual qualifications, and the employer should ask the same questions of all applicants for the same job. A past employer can *provide* only limited information on a past employee. A prospective employer can *conduct* a background check if the information is *strictly* job related. A prospective employer can *check* an applicant's credit history if an applicant's personal finances are job related, such as if the applicant will *handle* large sums of money. Certain types of pre-employment tests are legal, including job-related intelligence and skills tests or drug tests.

Employment

Fill in the blanks to complete the sentences:

16. The government has _____ laws to provide for a safe and fair workplace.
17. Laws _____ the rights of the worker.
18. Workers have the _____ to a safe workplace.
19. Employers know to keep within legal boundaries when _____ employees.
20. A basic law covers _____ wage.
21. Mary was so nervous during her _____ that she was sure she had made a bad impression on her prospective employer, but she was hired for the job.
22. _____ employers have to stay within strict guidelines when interviewing.
23. Hiring _____ have changed to reflect the changing social conditions in this country.
24. Employers can ask questions only about a person's _____ for the job.
25. _____ an interview has become complicated for employers.
26. Past employers are limited in what information they can _____ on a past employee.
27. Any search for information must be _____ job related.
28. Some firms perform a background _____ to get specialized information.
29. If a new employee will _____ large sums of money, employers can conduct a finance check.
30. People who feel they have been _____ because of their race, sex, or beliefs may be able to sue their employers.

Success with Legal Words

Answer Key

1. to approve or make into law
2. to defend against harm
3. legal entitlement
4. to engage the services of
5. the least possible
6. conversation arranged to discuss a matter
7. expected
8. habit, routine
9. ability that suits a person to a task
10. to direct the course of something
11. to supply
12. rigid
13. to make sure that something is correct
14. to deal with
15. to act with prejudice against
16. passed
17. protect
18. right
19. hiring
20. minimum
21. interview
22. prospective
23. practices
24. qualifications
25. conducting
26. provide
27. strictly
28. check
29. handle
30. discriminated against

14 Estate

Match each word or phrase to its meaning:

1.	to own	money paid or to be paid for something
2.	to encompass	consequence
3.	method	to lessen
4.	living will	to pass the ownership of the property to another
5.	to reduce	to count goods and possessions
6.	expense	a manner of accomplishing something
7.	outright	enough
8.	to convey	objective
9.	ramification	to possess
10.	power of attorney	to maintain
11.	to inventory	will in which signer asks not to be kept alive by medical support if terminally ill
12.	goal	necessary basis of something
13.	to preserve	to include
14.	adequate	completely
15.	cornerstone	document authorizing someone to act as another's attorney or agent

Success with Legal Words

Can you figure out the meanings of the italicized words in the following passages?

Conversation One:

MR. CHRISTIANO: As you plan your estate, you'll need to both distribute your property and *reduce* after-death *expenses* for your heirs.

MR. FRANZ: Yes, I'd like for them to pay the smallest amount of estate taxes possible.

Conversation Two:

MR. CHRISTIANO: Let's look at parts of your estate that affect you while you are still alive. You should think about a *living will* and a *power of attorney* agreement.

MR. FRANZ: I'll need somebody I trust who knows my wishes to handle those matters.

Short Talk:

The term "estate" means all the property a person *owns*. Estate planning *encompasses* a number of *methods* that people of all ages can use to determine where their estate will go after they die. It can significantly *reduce* the after-death *expenses* heirs pay from the estate. Writing a will is a *cornerstone* of the estate-planning process. Estate planning can also include making *outright* gifts before death, trusts, and other ways to *convey* property to others. In order to practice optimal estate planning, you should evaluate tax *ramifications* to decrease the number of assets that will be probated after you die. You should plan for your death by creating an *inventory* of your property, valuing it, and deciding whom you want to have it after you die. The *goal* of estate planning is to *preserve* your assets while you are alive with *adequate* insurance, durable *powers of attorney*, and a *living will*.

Estate

Fill in the blanks to complete the sentences:

16. You can _____ the amount of taxes your heirs will pay.
17. Wills are the basic _____ of the estate planning process.
18. If you don't want to be kept alive on a life support system if you fall into a coma, be sure to make out a _____.
19. Make sure your clients have _____ insurance to cover their potential medical costs.
20. Good estate planning _____ a number of methods that protect your assets.
21. By _____ property to an heir, you can avoid estate taxes and reduce the amount of your estate subject to probate.
22. A _____ agreement will allow someone else to act as your agent.
23. There are a number of legal _____ available for minimizing the number of assets that will go through probate.
24. Making an _____ gift to an heir is one way to reduce what goes through probate.
25. Heirs pay many _____ from the estate.
26. Considering the tax _____ to the estate can help your client decide if she wants to plan her estate.
27. The _____ of estate planning is to organize a client's estate both in life and after death.
28. People need enough assets to _____ their accustomed standard of living.
29. Your property is considered to be all the real estate and possessions you _____.
30. Your client can start the estate-planning process at home by taking an _____ of his property and assigning a value to it.

Success with Legal Words

Answer Key

1. to possess
2. to include
3. a manner of accomplishing something
4. will in which signer asks not to be kept alive by medical support if terminally ill
5. to lessen
6. money paid or to be paid for something
7. completely
8. to pass the ownership of the property to another
9. consequence
10. document authorizing someone to act as another's attorney or agent
11. to count goods and possessions
12. objective
13. to maintain
14. enough
15. necessary basis of something
16. reduce
17. cornerstone
18. living will
19. adequate
20. encompasses
21. conveying
22. power of attorney
23. methods
24. outright
25. expenses
26. ramifications
27. goal
28. preserve
29. own
30. inventory

15 Harassment

Match each word or phrase to its meaning:

1.	conduct	direct challenge
2.	to intimidate	definitive and decisive act
3.	hostile	liable
4.	behavior	to frighten someone to make him do something
5.	assault	diffused through every part of
6.	intolerable	to refuse to take notice of
7.	to prevent	manner of conducting oneself
8.	pervasive	unbearable
9.	confrontation	to die down, lessen
10.	determination	standard of behavior
11.	to disapprove	to object to
12.	to abate	physical attack
13.	responsible	wounds
14.	to ignore	unfriendly, malevolent
15.	injury	to stop from happening

Success with Legal Words

Can you figure out the meanings of the italicized words in the following passages?

Conversation One:

STACY: My harasser's supervisor *ignored* my complaint.

NINA: Make sure the company management knows about your struggle. That will make them *responsible* if they don't put a stop to the *behavior*.

Conversation Two:

STACY: My boss keeps touching me in a sexual way. It's really *intolerable*. Where do I stand legally?

NINA: Incidences of touching will give you more grounds for a legal claim than if the harassment solely involved comments.

Short Talk:

Sexual harassment is any unwelcome sexual advance or *conduct* on the job that creates an *intimidating*, offensive, or *hostile* working environment. Sexually harassing behavior ranges from repeated offensive or belittling jokes to sexual *assault*. The U.S. Supreme Court ruled in 1986 that sexual harassment is a form of job discrimination and held it to be illegal. Legally, no clear definition of *pervasive* conduct exists. If a person feels that she is being harassed, counsel her to tell the harasser to stop. Direct *confrontation* is a good first approach that can *prevent* further offenses. It is a tangible assertion of the woman's *disapproval* of and *determination* to stop the behavior. If the harasser persists, your client should put her objections in writing to the harasser or his supervisor. If the harassment still does not *abate*, tell the employer about the behavior. Employers can be held *responsible* if they *ignore* harassment complaints. If attempts to produce a resolution fail, your client may file a suit for *injuries* or punitive damages.

Harassment

Fill in the blanks to complete the sentences:

16. Sexual harassment can be used _____ people into feeling they have to do something to keep their jobs.

17. If it knows about the situation, the employer cannot legally _____ the problem.

18. Sexual harassment is unwelcome sexual _____ in the workplace.

19. Sexual _____ is the most severe form of harassment.

20. Confronting the harasser is often a good way _____ further behavior.

21. Verbal and written confrontation demonstrates the woman's clear _____ to end the behavior.

22. A sexual harassment victim can sue for emotional or psychological _____ resulting from the harassment.

23. It is claimed that sexual harassment creates a _____ environment.

24. A woman can merely shake her head to show her _____ of sexually harassing behavior.

25. If confronting the harasser does not cause the situation _____, take action with the employer.

26. Cases have shown how sexual harassment makes the workplace _____ for the person being harassed.

27. You can _____ the harasser nonverbally, verbally, and/or in writing.

28. Repeatedly telling belittling jokes can constitute harassing _____.

29. The law is unclear on what kinds of behavior constitute _____ conduct and how often they must occur.

30. Greater results can be obtained if the employer is made _____ for the harasser's behavior.

Success with Legal Words

Answer Key

1. standard of behavior
2. to frighten someone to make him do something
3. unfriendly, malevolent
4. manner of conducting oneself
5. physical attack
6. unbearable
7. to stop from happening
8. diffused through every part
9. direct challenge
10. definitive and decisive act
11. to object to
12. to die down, lessen
13. liable
14. to refuse to take notice of
15. wound
16. to intimidate
17. ignore
18. conduct
19. assault
20. to prevent
21. determination
22. injuries
23. hostile
24. disapproval
25. to abate
26. intolerable
27. confront
28. behavior
29. pervasive
30. responsible

16 Health

Match each word or phrase to its meaning:

1.	to involve	to be one of a group or project
2.	aspect	to agree to
3.	to assert	based on possessing an understanding
4.	treatment	without taking into account
5.	to consent	prospect of recovery
6.	to explain	habitual performance of a procedure
7.	prognosis	in less than perfect condition
8.	to participate	to engage in
9.	policy	formal consent
10.	informed	to provide with credentials
11.	routine	to state forcefully
12.	impaired	program of dealing medically with a person
13.	regardless	a detail or factor
14.	to accredit	management principle
15.	permission	to make understandable

Success with Legal Words

Can you figure out the meanings of the italicized words in the following passages?

Conversation One:

CARMEN: My mother can't understand her doctor's *explanations*. Her English isn't very good.

OTTO: As a patient, it's her right to be able to understand what she is being told about her *treatment*. Maybe the hospital can provide an interpreter.

Conversation Two:

POLLY: When our son was in the emergency room, the hospital performed a procedure on him that's against our religion, and they didn't seek our *permission* to do it. Can we take action against the hospital?

RITA: Probably not. In an emergency situation, the hospital isn't required to get the *consent* of the patient or of the family to act. It's against hospital *policy*.

Short Talk:

In today's health care environment, consumers must be *involved* in all *aspects* of their health care and ready to *assert* their rights. Patients have the right to understand any *treatment* their doctor suggests and their *prognosis*, as well as the right to *consent* to or refuse any procedure or to *participate* in any medical research project. *Routine* procedures, such as blood draws or inoculations, do not require a signed consent form. If the patient cannot make medical decisions for him or herself because of temporary or permanent *impairment*, the law provides that a close relative can give or withhold consent. State and federal laws require that all public and private hospitals treat anyone with a medical emergency, *regardless* of whether or not that patient is able to pay. If they do not, they risk government fines, lawsuits, and loss of *accreditation*.

Health

Fill in the blanks to complete the sentences:

16. A patient can elect _____ or refrain from being included in a research study.
17. If a patient is _____ and thus cannot understand an informed consent form, a family member must sign in place of the patient.
18. Decisions about the _____ plan should involve the patient.
19. The doctor is required _____ the care plan in language the patient can understand.
20. Patients will read and sign an _____ consent agreement that shows they understand and are willing to participate in a procedure.
21. The patient's right to understand his or her long-term _____ is protected.
22. Patients who feel they have been treated unfairly can complain to the organizations that _____ the hospital.
23. Many _____ of health care decision making demand the patient's input.
24. Before a significant procedure can begin, a patient must give its _____.
25. The Patient's Bill of Rights is part of the operating _____ of each hospital.
26. Patients must give their _____ before a major procedure can begin.
27. _____ procedures are simple and do not require a signed consent.
28. An emergency room must treat any patient who arrives, _____ of his or her ability to pay.
29. The patient has to speak out and _____ his rights.
30. The contemporary medical environment expects patients to be _____ in decisions affecting their health.

Success with Legal Words

Answer Key

1. to engage in
2. a detail or factor
3. to state forcefully
4. program of dealing medically with a person
5. to agree to
6. to make understandable
7. prospect of recovery
8. to be one of a group or project
9. management principle
10. based on possessing an understanding
11. habitual performance of a procedure
12. in less than perfect condition
13. without taking into account
14. to provide with credentials
15. formal consent
16. to participate
17. impaired
18. treatment
19. to explain
20. informed
21. prognosis
22. accredit
23. aspects
24. consent
25. policy
26. permission
27. routine
28. regardless
29. assert
30. involved

17 Immigration I

Match each word or phrase to its meaning:

1. to govern — interrelated principles, laws, rules
2. conditions — to change
3. to enter — to ask for something
4. to vary — lasting indefinitely
5. to depend — to deal with
6. to apply — to own or keep
7. to cover — to go in
8. criteria — period of time before marriage
9. to screen — to give someone the right to something
10. permanent — to rule
11. to entitle — standards by which something can be judged
12. to hold — to happen
13. to occur — to rely on
14. system — agreed way in which something takes place
15. engagement — to examine something to see if it is suitable

Success with Legal Words

Can you figure out the meanings of the italicized words in the following passages?

Conversation One:

MANUEL: My brother wants to come to this country, too. How should he start the *application* process for a visa?

ELLA: In order to *enter* the United States, he'll need to get a visa in his own country.

Conversation Two:

MANUEL: How long will it take to get a visa? He may try to enter as a student.

ELLA: I don't know—it *varies*. Student visas are handled under a different *system*.

Short Talk:

The U.S. Immigration and Naturalization Service (INS) *governs* who can and cannot *enter* the United States and under what conditions. The length of time required to get a visa *depends* on what kind of visa is being *applied* for, what country the applicant comes from, his or her job skills, and whether or not he or she already has family in the United States. Nonimmigrant visas *cover* people for about six months to a year. Immigrant visas cover those who want to live and work in the United States. The INS has certain *criteria* it uses to *screen* aliens who apply for visas. To stay *permanently* in the United States, an alien must have an immigrant work visa or "green card." The green card does not *entitle* the *holder* to citizenship. If a non-U.S. citizen is *engaged* to marry a U.S. citizen, the non-U.S. citizen can enter on a nonimmigrant visa under many circumstances. Once this individual has entered the United States, the marriage must *occur* within 90 days.

Immigration I

Fill in the blanks to complete the sentences:

16. Factors like work history, criminal record, and health status are used to _____ candidates.

17. Not everyone who wants _____ the country can get in.

18. Certain people can enter this country simply because they are _____ to U.S. citizens.

19. More people _____ for visas than receive them.

20. Non-U.S. citizens can get green cards under certain _____.

21. Each country has laws that _____ important matters like immigration.

22. Different rules _____ different types of visas.

23. Each type of visa has its own _____ for which applicants are accepted.

24. If an alien wants to remain _____ in this country, he or she must apply for a green card.

25. _____ a green card does not entitle one to citizenship.

26. The chances of getting a visa _____ on different factors, such as job skills.

27. If an alien is marrying a U.S. citizen as the basis for entering the country, the marriage must _____ soon after arrival.

28. Different visa _____ cover work and educational visas.

29. The rules pertaining to immigration _____ from country to country.

30. Those who hold green cards are _____ to various government benefits provided to all residents of the United States.

Success with Legal Words

Answer Key

1. to rule
2. interrelated principles, laws, rules
3. to go in
4. to change
5. to rely on
6. to ask for something
7. to deal with
8. standards by which something can be judged
9. to examine something to see if it is suitable
10. lasting indefinitely
11. to give someone the right to something
12. to own or keep
13. to happen
14. agreed way in which something takes place
15. period of time before marriage
16. screen
17. to enter
18. engaged
19. apply
20. conditions
21. govern
22. cover
23. criteria
24. permanently
25. holding
26. depend
27. occur
28. systems
29. vary
30. entitled

18 Immigration II

Match each word or phrase to its meaning:

1. quota — handling of forms and reports
2. to maintain — adept
3. to allot — system
4. to sponsor — important event
5. paperwork — to preserve
6. to complete — to ask a higher authority to reverse a decision
7. to certify — to have at one's disposal
8. milestone — to insist upon
9. process — to design for a specific purpose
10. to command — maximum number allowed or mandated
11. to intend — to give up voluntarily
12. proficient — to finish
13. to require — to vouch for the suitability of a candidate
14. to waive — to make an official declaration
15. to appeal — to distribute

Success with Legal Words

Can you figure out the meanings of the italicized words in the following passages?

Conversation One:

YURI: How hard will it be for me to get a green card?

AMPARO: It depends on the number of slots *allotted* each year to your birth country.

YURI: I'll have to check the list of available visas to learn how many slots are still open.

Conversation Two:

ABIMBOLA: I want my employer to *sponsor* me for permanent residency. Is that lots of *paperwork*?

AMPARO: Well, it starts with a labor *certification* process. There are different categories and *quotas* depending on your background and the job you have, so there is lots of paperwork.

Short Talk:

The U.S. maintains *quotas* that *allot* more visas to some countries than to others. The quota system is based on an alien's country of birth, not of citizenship. The immigration system allows for family and employee *sponsorship*. *Paperwork* is completed with the INS. Many immigrants want to become naturalized U.S. citizens. Five years after immigrating, aliens can begin the citizenship *process*. After this *milestone*, you can begin the process by completing an application with the INS. The INS will conduct an interview to make certain the alien has a *command* of the English language, *intends* to live in the United States, and is of good moral character. Under certain conditions, such as age, the INS may *waive* the English *proficiency requirement*. If the citizenship application is denied, the alien can *appeal* in federal court.

Immigration II

Fill in the blanks to complete the sentences:

16. Families and employers can _____ an immigrant for a visa.
17. As with all government operations, there is _____ required for a visa.
18. Being in the country five years is a _____ event.
19. Usually, people go to a government building, like a courthouse, to _____ their paperwork.
20. Check the _____ for your profession to see how many visas are left in your category.
21. You can _____ a citizenship rejection in court.
22. English language _____ will be tested on the citizenship test.
23. The citizenship _____ can take a long time to complete.
24. In certain circumstances, the government can _____ the language requirement on the application.
25. The citizenship application will test an applicant's _____ of the language.
26. The government _____ a list of visa quotas for different categories.
27. The government will _____ that the job for which your employer is sponsoring you meets certain criteria.
28. The applicant must state whether or not she _____ to live permanently in the United States on the citizenship application.
29. An applicant for citizenship may be _____ to have a job or speak the language well.
30. Visas are _____ based on birth country, not the country of citizenship.

Success with Legal Words

Answer Key

1. maximum number allowed or mandated
2. to preserve
3. to distribute
4. to vouch for the suitability of a candidate
5. handling of forms and reports
6. to finish
7. to make an official declaration
8. important event
9. system
10. to have at one's disposal
11. to design for a specific purpose
12. adept
13. to insist upon
14. to give up voluntarily
15. to ask a higher authority to reverse a decision
16. sponsor
17. paperwork
18. milestone
19. complete
20. quota
21. appeal
22. proficiency
23. process
24. waive
25. command
26. maintains
27. certify
28. intends
29. required
30. allotted

19 Investment

Match each word or phrase to its meaning:

1. to allege — to expose oneself to danger or harm
2. remedial — to deceive someone so as to obtain something illegally
3. misconduct — not suitable
4. to obey — to forbid
5. to risk — to bring someone to court to answer a criminal charge
6. punitive — illegal or harmful action
7. to bar — free, not controlled by anyone
8. to obtain — to come between two things
9. to prosecute — to state that something has happened
10. to defraud — dealing with legal principles
11. to intervene — to settle a dispute between parties without going to court
12. inappropriate — to do what one has been told to do
13. arbitration — to succeed in possessing something
14. independent — corrective
15. substantive — inflicting punishment

Success with Legal Words

Can you figure out the meanings of the italicized words in the following passages?

Conversation One:

JACK: I'm convinced my investor did not act in my best interest. I think she should be *prosecuted*.

MARCY: Don't take the *risk* of trying to represent yourself. Securities law is very complicated.

Conversation Two:

MARCY: If you take a private response to your broker about her *alleged misconduct*, the securities regulators will investigate the case and take action.

JACK: I want to get her fired!

MARCY: You might be able to do that. The SEC might also *bar* her firm from engaging in some aspects of the securities industry, or take other *punitive* action against it.

Short Talk:

The Securities and Exchange Commission (SEC) laws provide for responses to *allegations* of wrongdoing in the securities industry. Public response takes the form of a *remedial* action. Remedial actions stop and prevent future *misconduct*. Brokers failing to *obey* the court order *risk* imprisonment or other *punitive* action. The last public action is an order to give back illegally *obtained* money or to pay fines and penalties. Violators may also be required to return money to *defrauded* investors. The SEC cannot directly *intervene* in disputes. In a private response, investors try to recover losses they allege were caused by *inappropriate* activities, in federal or state court or through *arbitration*. Arbitration is a way to resolve disputes outside the court system. *Independent* arbitrators make *substantive* decisions about cases based upon the facts.

Investment

Fill in the blanks to complete the sentences:

16. _____ is usually less expensive and time consuming than court.

17. The SEC can _____ an investor from practicing some or all aspects of the industry.

18. If an investor _____ money illegally, he or she can be forced to return it.

19. Criminal authorities will _____ a serious offense.

20. An attempt to _____ an investor is a prosecutable offense.

21. A _____ action can be imposed to punish misconduct.

22. Failure to obey a court order means _____ imprisonment.

23. The SEC does not directly _____ between an investor and a brokerage house.

24. If a broker or brokerage fails _____ a court order, it will suffer a serious penalty.

25. To recover losses due to _____ activities by an investor, your client will have to go to court or to arbitration.

26. Arbiters make _____ decisions based on the facts they elicit.

27. Courts can take _____ action designed to prevent future occurrences.

28. If your client _____ misconduct, securities law provides for responses.

29. An _____ arbiter will hear each side impartially and render a decision.

30. Criminal authorities may investigate serious _____.

Success with Legal Words

Answer Key

1. to state that something has happened
2. corrective
3. illegal or harmful action
4. to do what one has been told to do
5. to expose oneself to danger or harm
6. inflicting punishment
7. to forbid
8. to succeed in possessing something
9. to bring someone to court to answer a criminal charge
10. to deceive someone so as to obtain something illegally
11. to come between two things
12. not suitable
13. to settle a dispute between two parties without going to court
14. free, not controlled by anyone
15. dealing with legal principles
16. arbitration
17. bar
18. obtains
19. prosecute
20. defraud
21. remedial
22. risking
23. intervene
24. to obey
25. inappropriate
26. substantive
27. punitive
28. alleges
29. independent
30. misconduct

20 Juveniles

Match each word or phrase to its meaning:

1.	to deal with	to stand behind; to cover the costs of living for
2.	to commit	relationship of result to cause
3.	to define	young criminal who commits minor criminal acts
4.	to support	immoral, low, evil
5.	to take into account	to state the precise meaning of
6.	to accuse	ability to receive or absorb
7.	delinquent	act that is against the law
8.	consequence	to be concerned with
9.	depraved	capacity for rational thought
10.	capacity	to consider
11.	juvenile	to make someone a fit member of society
12.	offense	to do, to carry out
13.	to detain	to hold a person so that he cannot leave
14.	reason	to charge with a crime
15.	to rehabilitate	minor child, usually under the age of 16

Success with Legal Words

Can you figure out the meanings of the italicized words in the following passages?

Conversation One:

MRS. LEVINE: Our son's been *accused* of robbing a liquor store. He's been *detained* by the police!

MR. BEAUREGARD: If your son is under 18 and still lives at home, he will most likely be treated as a *juvenile*.

Conversation Two:

MR. BEAUREGARD: The judge has decided your son knew the *consequences* of his *actions*.

MRS. LEVINE: That's ridiculous! My son is a sweet, innocent boy, not some *depraved* career criminal.

MR. BEAUREGARD: Well, unfortunately, it looks like he may be treated as an adult if they find him guilty.

Short Talk:

State laws *dealing* with crimes *committed* by a *juvenile* vary. A juvenile is generally *defined* as a child under the age of 18 who lives with or is *supported* by his or her parents. Juvenile law is different and *takes into account* that most young people cannot reason like adults. If a juvenile is *accused* of *delinquent* behavior, and a judge decides he or she can tell right from wrong and knows the *consequences* of his or her *actions*, the child will be accused of a crime. Most states agree that a child under the age of 8 or 9 does not have the mental *capacity* to commit a crime. While young children may understand that what they are doing is wrong, they do not understand the legal consequences of their behavior. If the child's *offense* is serious, the court can *detain* him or her in a juvenile center. The juvenile system tries to *rehabilitate*, not to punish.

Juveniles

Fill in the blanks to complete the sentences:

16. States have separate systems _____ juvenile offenders.

17. When children _____ crimes, the juvenile court system handles the case.

18. A child is _____ as a person under 18 years of age.

19. If a minor is under 18, _____ by and living with his parents, he is usually considered a juvenile.

20. The law _____ that children cannot reason like adults.

21. A judge will _____ a juvenile of a crime if the judge decides the juvenile understood the consequences of what he or she did.

22. A rising number of juveniles are being accused of _____ behavior.

23. If the child understood the _____ of his behavior, he may be accused of a crime.

24. Few juvenile offenders can be considered hardened, _____ criminals.

25. Children under 8 or 9 do not have the _____ to understand the consequences of their actions.

26. If the juvenile's _____ is serious, he or she can be detained in a juvenile center.

27. Serious offenders are not free to walk the streets—they may be _____ for prolonged periods.

28. Most minors cannot _____ like adults.

29. The juvenile court system tries to _____ minors, not punish them.

30. _____ are considered by most states to be persons under the age of 16.

Success with Legal Words

Answer Key

1. to be concerned with
2. to do, to carry out
3. to state the precise meaning of
4. to stand behind, to cover costs of living for
5. to consider
6. to charge with a crime
7. young criminal who commits minor criminal acts
8. relationship of result to cause
9. immoral, low, evil
10. ability to receive or absorb
11. minor child, usually under the age of 16
12. act that is against the law
13. to hold a person so that he cannot leave
14. capacity for rational thought
15. to make someone a fit member of society
16. to deal with
17. commit
18. defined
19. supported
20. takes into account
21. accuse
22. delinquent
23. consequences
24. depraved
25. capacity
26. offense
27. detained
28. reason
29. rehabilitate
30. juveniles

21 Landlords

Match each word or phrase to its meaning:

1. to assure   capable of being put into effect
2. premises   within the bounds of common sense
3. notice   disagreement
4. to guarantee   to come in without invitation
5. reasonable   building and the land it stands on
6. term   to make two sides come to an agreement
7. to evict   to give up something voluntarily
8. practical   to promise that something will happen
9. to abandon   to injure
10. to force   to inform confidently
11. conflict   agreement in which both sides give way
12. to mediate   to force someone to leave a property
13. compromise   information officially passed on
14. to violate   to produce by effort
15. to intrude   condition of a contract

Success with Legal Words

Can you figure out the meanings of the italicized words in the following passages?

Conversation One:

LOUISE: My landlord wants to stay with us while she's in town, although we rent the whole house.

WALTER: That is not a *reasonable* request. She can't *intrude* on your privacy whenever she feels like it.

Conversation Two:

GRANT: I want to inspect my rental unit and my tenants won't let me in. Can I *evict* them?

KATHLEEN: Are they otherwise good tenants?

GRANT: Yes. They pay the rent on time and I get no complaints from the neighbors.

KATHLEEN: I urge you to consider *mediation* to get them to understand your point of view.

Short Talk:

States *guarantee* tenants *reasonable* privacy rights against a landlord's *intrusions*. A landlord can enter rental *premises* after giving the tenants *reasonable notice* (usually considered 24 hours). Shorter notice may be allowed if it is not *practical* to provide the required notice. Except in emergency cases, *abandonment*, and by invitation by the tenant, a landlord can enter only during normal business hours. A landlord cannot *force* entry except in cases of emergency. If a landlord has a *conflict* with a tenant who otherwise meets the terms of the lease, he or she should try to *mediate* the situation. If this attempt at *compromise* does not work, *eviction* for *violating* the lease is a landlord's last recourse. A tenant can ask for *assurances* that a landlord's aggressive conduct will not be repeated.

Landlords

Fill in the blanks to complete the sentences:

16. State laws _____ renters reasonable privacy against intrusions by landlords.

17. If a landlord is having a severe problem with an otherwise satisfactory tenant, _____ should take place.

18. A landlord must give reasonable _____ before entering a unit.

19. Only in emergency situations can a landlord enter the _____ without the renter's permission.

20. It is easier and cheaper to reach a _____ with a tenant than to evict him.

21. _____ is when the tenant moves out without giving notice.

22. A tenant must live up to the _____ of the lease.

23. Sometimes it is not _____ for landlords to give reasonable notice to enter the premises.

24. Entering without permission may be considered a _____ of privacy by your tenant.

25. A landlord cannot _____ except in emergency situations.

26. Unless there is a true emergency, a landlord should not try _____ entry.

27. _____ notice is usually considered 24 hours.

28. Often, third parties can resolve _____ between landlords and renters.

29. A tenant can ask for a landlord's _____ that improper entry will not be repeated.

30. A landlord can _____ a tenant after attempts to resolve the problems fail.

Success with Legal Words

Answer Key

1. to inform confidently
2. building and the land it stands on
3. information officially passed on
4. to promise that something will happen
5. within the bounds of common sense
6. condition of a contract
7. to force someone to leave a property
8. capable of being put into effect
9. to give up something voluntarily
10. to produce by effort
11. disagreement
12. to make two sides come to an agreement
13. agreement in which both sides give way
14. to injure
15. to come in without invitation
16. guarantee
17. mediation
18. notice
19. premises
20. compromise
21. abandonment
22. terms
23. practical
24. violation
25. intrude
26. to force
27. reasonable
28. conflicts
29. assurance
30. evict

22 Patents

Match each word or phrase to its meaning:

1. product — to create the first version of
2. to manufacture — to change the form or appearance of an original model
3. to deceive — to cause to draw near
4. to encourage — only
5. innovation — to make
6. to transform — to be the first to learn or observe something
7. to attract — to inspire to continue on a chosen course
8. capital — state of being hidden
9. to invent — material article
10. to discover — happening while an application is on file
11. prototype — material wealth available to make more wealth
12. to contribute — to lie to, trick
13. sole — to add to
14. secrecy — that which is newly introduced
15. pending

Success with Legal Words

Can you figure out the meanings of the italicized words in the following passages?

Conversation One:

DR. RANDALL: I've come up with an *innovative* anticancer drug. Can you help me patent it?

MS. PARKER: Only those attorneys recognized by the Patent Office can represent an *inventor*.

Conversation Two:

DR. RANDALL: I can't wait to protect this product, so I can *attract* investors to get my business started.

MR. SINGH: Be patient. The review process takes time to complete, and you need to send in a *prototype*.

Short Talk:

Look on almost any *product* in your house or office, and you will find the phrase "patent pending." *Manufacturers* use this to inform the public that an application for patent is pending in the U.S. Patent and Trademarks Office. The law imposes a fine on those who use these terms falsely *to deceive* the public. Patents *encourage* inventors—without the protection that patents provide, we would not have the *innovations* that have *transformed* society. Patents make it possible for inventors to market, sell, and license their inventions, and to attract necessary *capital*. Patents are granted for new and useful *inventions* and *discoveries* related to processes, machines, manufactured articles, medications, and improvements of articles already holding patents. To be protected, you must complete a patent application, describing the invention and providing a *prototype*. Patent applications are maintained in strict *secrecy* until the government issues a patent. If one person has provided all the ideas of the invention, the person who *contributes* the ideas is the *sole* inventor and holds the patent.

Patents

Fill in the blanks to complete the sentences:

16. Patents allow firms to _____ an article and retain the right to make or sell it.

17. The patent process protects ideas, so the person who invents the product is the _____ holder of the patent, even if there are financial backers.

18. If you _____ a new product, you can patent it.

19. Patent _____ means an application is on file in the Patent Office for that product.

20. Because of patent protection, inventors can _____ an innovation into a marketable product.

21. The market protection a patent provides makes it possible for inventors _____ financial backers.

22. Patents make it possible for inventors to find _____ because the patent makes it impossible for anyone else to make or sell the product.

23. Patents _____ new ideas because those ideas are then protected.

24. _____, such as ways to improve existing drugs, can also be subject to patents.

25. When your client submits his or her application, remember to send a _____ if the patent is for a product or manufactured good.

26. Patents protect such _____ as new drugs, machines, and manufactured goods.

27. If one person _____ the ideas, and another the instructions for a product, the person whose idea it was earns the patent.

28. _____ on the market are protected by patents.

29. Until the patent is issued, the Patent Office holds the application in _____.

30. _____ the public by falsely claiming a patent is illegal.

Success with Legal Words

Answer Key

1. material article
2. to make
3. to lie to, trick
4. to inspire to continue on a chosen course
5. that which is newly introduced
6. to change the form or appearance of
7. to cause to draw near
8. material wealth available to make more wealth
9. to create the first version of
10. to be the first to learn or observe something
11. an original model
12. to add to
13. only
14. state of being hidden
15. happening while an application is on file
16. manufacture
17. sole
18. invent
19. pending
20. transform
21. to attract
22. capital
23. encourage
24. discoveries
25. prototype
26. innovations
27. contributes
28. products
29. secrecy
30. deceiving

23 Personal Injury

Match each word or phrase to its meaning:

1. to document — marked by regularity
2. to compensate — chance for advancement
3. victim — thing that has happened
4. technique — having material presence through the senses
5. consistent — request for payment of damages
6. detail — to pay for damages done
7. incident — to give an account in words
8. demand — behavior acquired by repetition
9. claim — method of accomplishing an aim
10. to sustain — to change
11. to describe — to record something to serve as proof
12. opportunity — to withstand, suffer
13. habit — something claimed as due
14. physical — person who suffers a crime or a wrong
15. to modify — small, specific part

Success with Legal Words

Can you figure out the meanings of the italicized words in the following passages?

Conversation One:

JANET: My neighbor told me he, too, could see that the stairs that I fell down needed repair.

GEORGE: *Document* that conversation today by sending him a note that *describes* your conversation.

Conversation Two:

JANET: I am going to take pictures of the accident site and have them developed immediately.

GEORGE: Make sure that the photo shop prints the date the photos were developed on the back of the photo. You'll be sure to get the *compensation* you want.

Short Talk:

There are a number of *techniques* you can use to help your client *demand* the most *compensation* possible after she or he has been the victim of an accident. *Document* the facts of the case early, *consistently*, and *in detail*. These notes will help build a case after the *incident*. Good written notes will help your client in the *claim* process and, if necessary, in the court process. Notes should give details of the injuries *sustained*, and their effect on the client's daily life. Your client should *describe* to his doctor all his injuries, even minor ones. The injuries will then be part of your client's medical record, which can be entered as evidence. Your client should also keep notes of work time lost; meetings, events, or engagements missed; vacations canceled; or job *opportunities* lost due to the accident. Keeping notes should become a *habit* for your client until the case is settled. *Physical* evidence should be found and collected immediately, before it can be *modified*. If you cannot get physical evidence, photographing it is a good idea.

Personal Injury

Fill in the blanks to complete the sentences:

16. Your client should _____ all his symptoms to the doctor so that they are included in his medical record.

17. Collect physical evidence promptly, before it can be _____.

18. Good records will help in your _____ for compensation.

19. You are entitled to compensation if you have been the _____ of an accident.

20. Any lost _____, either personal or professional, caused by the accident should be noted.

21. The more _____ the evidence is, the greater the chance that it will be useful.

22. Have your clients keep thorough track of any injuries or losses after the _____.

23. Have your client _____ every aspect of the case with notes, letters, and photographs.

24. If your client _____ injuries, even small injuries, make sure they are part of the medical record.

25. It can take months to settle a _____ against an insurance company.

26. _____ evidence is compelling, because it is visible and tangible.

27. Keeping good records _____ throughout the claims process is a good way to build evidence.

28. Many _____ for getting compensation, like keeping good notes, are just common sense.

29. Have your clients make a _____ of keeping good notes throughout the claims process.

30. Mrs. Tapp was unhappy with the _____ she received from the restaurant after the waiter spilled food on her.

Success with Legal Words

Answer Key

1. to record something to serve as proof
2. to pay for damages done
3. person who suffers a crime or wrong
4. method of accomplishing an aim
5. marked by regularity
6. small, specific part
7. thing which has happened
8. something claimed as due
9. request for payment of damages
10. to withstand, suffer
11. to give an account in words
12. chance for advancement
13. behavior acquired by repetition
14. having material presence through the senses
15. to change
16. describe
17. modified
18. demand
19. victim
20. opportunities
21. detailed
22. incident
23. document
24. sustains
25. claim
26. physical
27. consistently
28. techniques
29. habit
30. compensation

24 Social Security

Match each word or phrase to its meaning:

1.	insolvent	to make a provision for
2.	ingrained	yield produced
3.	dire	to meet the requirements for
4.	to project	amount taken from a paycheck
5.	to fund	to obtain payments of
6.	to cover	to change to make correspond to
7.	to collect	dreadful
8.	to qualify	to add a burden to
9.	mandatory	not able to pay debts
10.	deduction	to bring in
11.	to adjust	to extend out
12.	to weight	to decide
13.	return	deeply rooted
14.	to draw	to pay for
15.	to determine	required

Success with Legal Words

Can you figure out the meanings of the italicized words in the following passages?

Conversation One:

CARL: I don't know why you even bother to calculate how much you've paid into social security. It'll soon be *insolvent*, and you'll never see any of it back.

GILLIAN: The *projections* are pretty *dire*, but I think the government will find a way to keep the system going. It's so *ingrained* in our culture.

Conversation Two:

HARRY: I'm 62 now. Am I *qualified* to start *drawing* my social security benefits?

GILLIAN: You may want to wait until you are age 65. If you start *collecting* them now, the checks will be smaller.

Short Talk:

In addition to retirement income, social security taxes *fund* benefits not linked to retirement, such as disability income and Medicare. The social security system *covers* most jobs. Anyone who works long enough and earns enough salary can *collect* social security benefits. To *qualify* for benefits, an individual must accumulate 40 quarters' worth of credits. At the same time that people are earning credits, they are paying into the social security system. Employers take the payments as *mandatory* paycheck *deductions*. A social security formula *adjusted* for inflation *determines* the monthly paycheck, but in general, social security replaces 42 percent of lifetime earnings, assuming earnings were "average." The formula is *weighted* so that low-income workers receive a higher rate of *return* on their payments than highly paid workers. People can start *drawing* social security income as early as age 62, although most people wait until age 65.

Social Security

Fill in the blanks to complete the sentences:

16. The taxes that fund social security are _____, so everyone must pay.
17. The payment system is _____ to help those who made less income.
18. Employers take social security taxes as _____ directly from the paycheck.
19. Economists use extensive calculations _____ the long-term financial future of huge systems like social security.
20. Social security taxes also _____ disability programs.
21. The benefits of the social security system _____ most jobs.
22. If they work long enough and earn enough, Americans are entitled to _____ a social security check.
23. To get a good idea of how much income you will _____ each month, ask the Social Security Administration to estimate your benefits.
24. Many news stories predict that the social security system will be _____ by the early part of the 21st century.
25. Talk with the Social Security Administration at least a year before retirement to _____ the precise amount of the money you will collect.
26. To predict the payment, social security uses a formula _____ for inflation.
27. Although it is a relatively recent innovation, the social security benefit is _____ in our national culture.
28. People who made a lower wage receive a higher rate of _____ on their payments than those with higher incomes over the years.
29. To _____ for social security, people must have earned sufficient credits.
30. Some of the projections of the _____ financial status of the social security system are frightening.

Success with Legal Words

Answer Key

1. not able to pay debts
2. deeply rooted
3. dreadful
4. to extend out
5. to pay for
6. to make a provision for
7. to bring in
8. to meet the requirements for
9. required
10. amount taken from a paycheck
11. to change to make correspond to
12. to add a burden to
13. yield produced
14. to obtain payments of
15. to decide
16. mandatory
17. weighted
18. deductions
19. to project
20. fund
21. cover
22. collect
23. draw
24. insolvent
25. determine
26. adjusted
27. ingrained
28. return
29. qualify
30. dire

25 Taxes

Match each word or phrase to its meaning:

1.	to extend	overall, or before deductions
2.	services	serious or fatal accident
3.	uniform	to commit money in order to gain a financial return
4.	to consume	benefits
5.	income	state of affairs
6.	gross	relating to a specific person or thing
7.	to calculate	to use up
8.	source	to permit
9.	to invest	to release from liability
10.	particular	to give, to spread out
11.	to allow	to set down by particulars
12.	status	to determine by a mathematical process
13.	to exempt	consistent
14.	to itemize	origin
15.	casualty	a gain, usually measured in money

Success with Law Words

Can you figure out the meanings of the italicized words in the following passages?

Conversation One:

TED: It's your responsibility as a business owner to *calculate* the taxes you must pay.

AMANDA: That's why I'm hiring you, to make sure I don't pay any penalties.

Conversation Two:

AMANDA: My income tax is complicated this year. I should have paid estimated quarterly taxes, but I didn't.

TED: The tax code allows for different ways of *itemizing* deductions, depending on your *particular* circumstances. But you can probably expect your tax bill to be pretty high.

Short Talk:

Taxes, in the most *extended* sense, are contributions imposed by the government for the *services* of the state. The Constitution gives Congress the power to collect taxes, and makes the provision that taxes shall be *uniform* throughout the country. Taxes are divided into two classes: direct and indirect. Direct taxes are on land and real estate; indirect taxes are on articles of *consumption*. Congress also has the power to tax *income* annually. *Gross* income is all income from whatever *source*, and includes business income and capital assets, such as stock and bonds and *investment* property. Deductions for charitable contributions, home mortgage interest, certain taxes, interest expense, and losses from *casualty* or theft, for example, are taken. People can choose to *itemize* these deductions or take the standard deduction *allowed* by law. Each filer winds up with a specific amount that shows how much he or she owes, given income, filing *status*, and *exemptions*.

Taxes

Fill in the blanks to complete the sentences:

16. A _____ tax code sets tax policy across all the states.
17. Losses due to _____, such as the loss of a wrecked car, are deductible.
18. _____ taxes are generally taken out of each paycheck.
19. To _____ income taxes owed, start with your client's gross income.
20. Whatever the _____ of income, it is generally taxable.
21. The amount of deductions will vary by each _____ financial case.
22. Deductions are taken from the _____ income.
23. Your income filing _____ can vary depending upon whether you are married or single.
24. _____ income, whether it be property, securities, or stocks, is also taxable.
25. All persons are allowed a certain number of _____ from their income taxes.
26. The Constitution _____ to Congress the right to collect taxes.
27. People can _____ all their individual deductions or take the standard deduction.
28. Your taxes pay for the various _____ provided by the state.
29. _____ articles, such as clothing, are taxable.
30. The tax code _____ for a certain number of deductions from taxable income.

Success with Law Words

Answer Key

1. to give, to spread out
2. benefits
3. consistent
4. to use up
5. a gain, usually measured in money
6. overall, or before deductions
7. to determine by a mathematical process
8. origin
9. to commit money in order to gain a financial return
10. relating to a specific person or thing
11. to permit
12. state of affairs
13. to release from liability
14. to set down by particulars
15. serious or fatal accident
16. uniform
17. casualty
18. income
19. calculate
20. source
21. particular
22. gross
23. status
24. investment
25. exemptions
26. extends
27. itemize
28. services
29. consumable
30. allows

26 Trademarks

Match each word or phrase to its meaning:

1.	to designate	to put at risk
2.	original	to keep track of a process or activity
3.	to acquire	large-scale buying and selling of goods, trade
4.	use	distinguishing characteristics
5.	to register	made in good faith
6.	to jeopardize	to give permission to do that which would otherwise be illegal
7.	commerce	to specify
8.	to license	to go along with
9.	to monitor	service, practice of using
10.	bona fide	good reputation of a business and business contacts
11.	to accompany	area covered
12.	goodwill	not copied, first of its kind
13.	distinctive	a striking phrase used in advertisement
14.	scope	to gain possession of, usually through purchase
15.	slogan	to record on an official list

Success with Law Words

Can you figure out the meanings of the italicized words in the following passages?

Conversation One:

SHERRIE: I've come up with a great *slogan* for our product.

BOB: You should *register* the trademark to protect it.

SHERRIE: First, let's conduct a search so we know it is unique.

Conversation Two:

SHERRIE: We have registered a trademark for our clothing line, which I would like to *license*.

JOHN: That's possible as long as you protect yourself by *monitoring* the quality of the clothes made.

SHERRIE: Why is that so important?

JOHN: If the company turns out clothing that is drastically different from the *original* clothing made under the mark, the trademark is *jeopardized*.

Short Talk:

A trademark *designates* the source of a product. Under U.S. law, companies and individuals *acquire* trademarks by *use*. To *enhance* their rights, individuals or companies will *register* their marks. They file a federal trademark application based on either the trademark owner's actual use of the mark or on a *bona fide* intent to use the mark in *commerce*. Companies can *license* a trademark to a third party, as long as they *monitor* quality control. Failure to do so may result in loss of rights to the mark. Companies can sell or assign their trademarks as long as the *goodwill* represented by the mark *accompanies* the transfer. The *distinctiveness* in which a company uses trademark affects the *scope* of the protection. Once a company or an individual obtains a trademark, it is valid for 10 years.

Trademarks

Fill in the blanks to complete the sentences:

16. Usually, companies acquire trademarks through _____.

17. The more _____ a trademark, the easier it is to protect it.

18. The goodwill of a trademark must _____ the assignment of the mark.

19. The catchy _____ in the ad helped to sell large quantities of the product.

20. The poor quality of the toys manufactured by the factory to which we licensed our trademark has _____ our reputation.

21. The true desire to use a trademark in _____ is sufficient cause to register it.

22. In order to _____ a trademark, it is generally considered sufficient to use it.

23. The businessman had a _____ intent to use the trademark, even though he never actually wound up manufacturing the product.

24. Companies _____ their marks with the federal government.

25. Companies must _____ the quality of a licensee using their mark.

26. If your client assigns or sells trademark rights, it must also transfer the _____ of the mark.

27. A company can _____ its mark to a third party.

28. Do a search to make sure the trademark is _____.

29. Trademarks _____ the source of a product.

30. The _____ of protection given to a mark depends on the distinctiveness of the mark.

Success with Law Words

Answer Key

1. to specify
2. not copied, first of its kind
3. to gain possession of, usually through purchase
4. service, practice of using
5. to record on an official list
6. to put at risk
7. large-scale buying and selling of goods, trade
8. to give permission to do that which would otherwise be illegal
9. to keep track of a process or activity
10. made in good faith
11. to go along with
12. good reputation of a business and business contacts
13. distinguishing characteristics
14. area covered
15. a striking phrase used in advertisement
16. use
17. distinctive
18. accompany
19. slogan
20. jeopardized
21. commerce
22. acquire
23. bona fide
24. register
25. monitor
26. goodwill
27. license
28. original
29. designate
30. scope

27 Traffic

Match each word or phrase to its meaning:

1. to track   ridiculous
2. severity   to collect
3. to contest   to come into court
4. to fine   to accuse
5. citation   to stop something for a time
6. absurd   dependable
7. to suspend   to levy a monetary punishment
8. to revoke   to affect someone or something
9. to gather   to monitor
10. reliable   value in excess of normal
11. to appear   to fight against
12. to dismiss   to cancel
13. to charge   official request to come to court
14. to influence   high degree of seriousness
15. premium   to discharge

Success with Law Words

Can you figure out the meanings of the italicized words in the following passages?

Conversation One:

DREW: My insurance company raised my rates. The cost is *absurd*.

LYDIA: Once you have a moving violation conviction on your record, companies often charge you a *premium* rate.

Conversation Two:

MRS. BAXTER: My husband will testify to support my side of the story.

MR. SUAREZ: That's not always foolproof. The judge may decide his testimony is not *reliable*. As your spouse, he is expected to be biased in your favor.

Short Talk:

States use a system called "points" to *track* the number and *severity* of moving violations of which an individual is convicted. Depending on the charge, a person will receive a certain number of points on his or her driving record. The more severe the *citation*, the more points the person is *fined*. Once a person accumulates *sufficient* points, his or her license can be *suspended* for a period of time or permanently *revoked*. If your client decides to *contest* a traffic ticket, you will have *to gather* evidence in support of the case. Traffic judges will take into account how *reliable* the witness is. A case will be settled in favor of the defendant if the citing police officer does not *appear* in court. If this happens to your client, *oppose* any request for a continuance the prosecution makes, and ask for immediate *dismissal* of all *charges*. The number of points on a driver's record can *influence* the rates insurance companies charge for auto insurance.

Traffic

Fill in the blanks to complete the sentences:

16. In addition to adding points to your license, a moving violation results in a _____.

17. A traffic judge will be concerned that any witness be _____ and unbiased.

18. A police officer will give a _____ for a moving vehicle violation.

19. If you have points on your driver's record, expect to pay a _____ insurance rate.

20. Every state has a computer system _____ moving vehicle violations.

21. The courts can _____ a driving license for a period of time.

22. If a violation is serious enough, or there are enough violations, the courts will _____ the privilege of driving.

23. _____ evidence thoughtfully in preparation for your court appearance.

24. In a traffic court, the police office who wrote the citation must also _____.

25. The driver considered the parking fine she had to pay _____ high.

26. If the police officer does not appear, the case against you should be _____.

27. Once there are points on the driving record, most insurance carriers will _____ higher rates.

28. Drivers with clean driving records may _____ their insurance companies to give them favorable rates.

29. The number of points assigned is tied to the _____ of the violation.

30. People who choose to _____ their traffic tickets must spend a lot of time in court proving their cases.

Success with Law Words

Answer Key

1. to monitor
2. high degree of seriousness
3. to fight against
4. to levy a monetary punishment
5. official request to come to court
6. ridiculous
7. to stop something for a time
8. to cancel
9. to collect
10. dependable
11. to come into court
12. to discharge
13. to accuse
14. to affect someone or something
15. value in excess of normal
16. fine
17. reliable
18. citation
19. premium
20. to track
21. suspend
22. revoke
23. gather
24. appear
25. absurdly
26. dismissed
27. charge
28. influence
29. severity
30. contest

28 Warranties

Match each word or phrase to its meaning:

1. amount — to not include
2. to compare — of great importance
3. characteristic — distinguishing feature
4. available — to make invalid
5. to expire — promise that something will function as it should
6. to exclude — action taken in advance to safeguard
7. damage — total quantity
8. manner — to use improperly
9. major — a way of doing something
10. warranty — general public estimation of something
11. to investigate — to note similarities or differences
12. precaution — accessible for use
13. reputation — to come to an end
14. to abuse — to inquire in detail
15. to cancel — impairment in usefulness or value

Success with Law Words

Can you figure out the meanings of the italicized words in the following passages?

Conversation One:

VANESSA: It's time for the car to be serviced.

LEO: We need to take the car to an authorized repair shop with a good *reputation* for the work to be covered by the *warranty*.

VANESSA: Oh, no—I just realized our warranty has *expired!*

Conversation Two:

EDITH: This dish got *damaged* in the microwave, although the salesperson told me it was microwave safe.

RAY: You should take it back to the store and ask for a refund. The salesperson gave you an implied *warranty* of fitness for microwave use.

Short Talk:

Warranties, also known as guarantees, are a seller's promise to stand behind a product. Warranties vary in the *amount* of coverage they provide, so *compare* warranties just as you compare the other *characteristics* of the product you are considering buying, especially when making *major* purchases. The law requires that warranties be *available* when a purchase is made. Certain types of repairs may be *excluded* from coverage. Most warranties require that you use the product in a certain *manner*, such as only in a home setting. Anything considered *abuse* of the product can *cancel* the warranty coverage. If a problem is not covered by the written warranty, *investigate* the protection available under the implied warranty. To minimize the chance of problems, take *precautions*, such as considering the *reputation* of the company offering the product.

Warranties

Fill in the blanks to complete the sentences:

16. The _____ covered by warranties varies greatly.
17. _____ that stem from a product's failure usually are not covered by the warranty.
18. If you do not use the product in a prescribed manner, the company can _____ the warranty.
19. You can _____ a company's record through the Better Business Bureau.
20. Almost all warranties _____, after which point they are no longer valid.
21. Exercise some common sense _____ before buying a product.
22. Consumers must _____ the different factors of coverage from manufacturer to manufacturer.
23. Warranties may dictate the _____ or location in which a product may be used.
24. Just as the _____ of a product vary, so do the features of a warranty.
25. Even _____ purchases are covered by warranties.
26. You'll be safer if you get a written _____ rather than an oral guarantee from a salesperson.
27. Most warranties _____ certain kinds of damages from coverage.
28. Warranties must be _____ for the consumer to read at the time of purchase.
29. Companies with established _____ generally have a better record of standing behind their products.
30. _____ or mistreating a product is a sure way to lose the coverage of the warranty.

Success with Law Words

Answer Key

1. total quantity
2. to note similarities and differences
3. distinguishing feature
4. accessible for use
5. to come to an end
6. to not include
7. impairment in usefulness or value
8. a way of doing something
9. of great importance
10. promise that something will function as it should
11. to inquire in detail
12. action taken in advance to safeguard
13. general public estimation of something
14. to use improperly
15. to make invalid
16. amount
17. damages
18. cancel
19. investigate
20. expire
21. precautions
22. compare
23. manner
24. characteristics
25. major
26. warranty
27. exclude
28. available
29. reputations
30. abusing

29 Wills

Match each word or phrase to its meaning:

1.	intestate	court that establishes validity of wills
2.	beneficiary	things of value that belong to someone
3.	executor	one who acts on behalf of someone else
4.	probate	to start
5.	representative	to acquire something from one who has died
6.	guardian	to choose someone for a job
7.	valid	to force someone by pressure
8.	to inherit	people who are left property in a will
9.	to distribute	person appointed by the court to manage the estate
10.	heirs	incontestable, binding
11.	assets	without a will
12.	to initiate	to give out
13.	to appoint	person who receives property when someone dies
14.	administrator	one who serves as an authorized agent for someone else, often a child
15.	to coerce	person who carries out the terms of the will

Success with Law Words

Can you figure out the meanings of the italicized words in the following passages?

Conversation One:

STEVE: Why do you want me to write my will? I have plenty of years left before I die.

HILARY: Every adult needs a will. You don't want your *heirs* to go through the hassle of your dying *intestate*.

Conversation Two:

SCOTT: My mother has died without making a will.

LAUREN: Now the *probate* court will have to decide who will *inherit* your mother's property and *distribute* it.

SCOTT: My sister is in financial difficulty and needs to access the money now.

LAUREN: That's a problem. Without a *valid* will, the *beneficiaries* cannot borrow against the *assets* without a transfer of ownership, which takes time to complete.

Short Talk:

Writing a will is the single most important thing people can do to control who will *receive* their property after they die. A will names an estate *executor* or legal *representative* to guide the estate through the *probate* process. A will should also name a *guardian* if there is a minor child involved. In the absence of a *valid* will, the state probate court decides who will inherit the property and *distributes* it to the legal heirs based on the laws of the state. Without a will, the heirs cannot sell or borrow against the deceased's *assets* without *initiating* legal transfership of ownership. The court will *appoint* an *administrator*. A will must be made of free will, without *coercion*, and written, signed, dated, and witnessed.

Wills

Fill in the blanks to complete the sentences:

16. The _____ are determined by a valid will, or by a judge if the deceased did not leave a will.

17. After probate is cleared, the proceeds of the will are _____ to the heirs.

18. The will is not valid if the person making it out was _____ into doing something he did not want to do.

19. The person named estate _____ usually charges for his or her services.

20. The estate executor is the legal _____ of the will through the probate process.

21. If the person making the will has a minor child, a _____ should be appointed in the will.

22. To borrow against the estate while it is in probate, the heirs must _____ a transfer of ownership.

23. A _____ will is critical to avoid time in the probate process.

24. When a person dies intestate, a state probate court will _____ an estate administrator.

25. A will states clearly who will _____ the property.

26. A will names the _____ of the deceased's property.

27. The _____ of the will guides it through the court system.

28. If a valid will was made, _____ should be straightforward.

29. If a person dies intestate, the heirs cannot use the _____ of the estate until they transfer ownership.

30. Those who die _____ risk having their property distributed in ways they might not have liked.

Success with Law Words

Answer Key

1. without a will
2. person who receives property when someone dies
3. person appointed by the court to manage the estate
4. court that establishes validity of wills
5. one who acts on behalf of someone else
6. one who serves as an authorized agent for someone else, often a child
7. incontestable, binding
8. to acquire something from someone who has died
9. to give out
10. people who are left property in a will
11. things of value that belong to someone
12. to start
13. to choose someone for a job
14. person who carries out the terms of the will
15. to force someone by pressure
16. heirs
17. distributed
18. coerced
19. administrator
20. representative
21. guardian
22. initiate
23. valid
24. appoint
25. inherit
26. beneficiaries
27. executor
28. probate
29. assets
30. intestate

30 Workplace

Match each word or phrase to its meaning:

1. security — to bother
2. to honor — to agree to
3. privacy — to say no
4. feedback — a hope for the future
5. to enable — to forbid
6. to refuse — working by degrees
7. to harass — to recognize and accept
8. to prohibit — unbiased
9. to acquiesce — to supply with the means to do something
10. expectation — seclusion from the intrusion of others
11. protocol — policies
12. grievance — freedom from doubt or anxiety
13. progressive — correct and standard procedure
14. impartial — information about the result of a process
15. guidelines — complaint made by employee to management

Success with Law Words

Can you figure out the meanings of the italicized words in the following passages?

Conversation One:

MR. GALLENBERGER: I'm glad that the company *honored* both sides in Mrs. Greenberg's *harassment* complaint.

MR. MCGUIRE: Yes, it shows that they are very concerned about maintaining *impartiality*.

Conversation Two:

MS. BURNS: Why do we have to worry about employee rights when we have so little extra money to spend?

MR. GALLENBERGER: Making sure that employees know their rights has been proven to reduce litigation for employee *grievances*.

Short Talk:

Employee rights fall into three categories: the right to job *security*, the right to fair treatment by the employer, and the right to fair treatment in the workplace. Fair treatment involves *honoring* the employees' right to *privacy*, and providing *feedback* regarding their performance to *enable* them to meet job *expectations*. Employee rights of privacy include the right to *refuse* a polygraph test or a drug test as a condition for employment. Employees have a right to *prohibit* release of any information about them if they do not *acquiesce*. An employee can demand the right to due process procedures, including consistent rules and *protocol* for making *grievances*. Employees are also entitled to a *progressive* system of discipline. Federal law entitles all employees to knowledge about workplace hazards, such as warnings about chemicals, and to *guidelines* for avoiding accidents.

Workplace

Fill in the blanks to complete the sentences:

16. An employee can _____ to take a drug test or a polygraph test as a condition of employment.

17. Giving _____ about job performance is not just good management, it's the law.

18. Managers should ensure that all employees are treated in an _____ manner at all times.

19. Employees have the right to know about the _____ process.

20. Employers need to _____ their employees' right to privacy.

21. Informing employees about _____, such as for handling hazardous waste, is the law.

22. Employees must _____ to the release of any information about them.

23. Federal laws ensure that an employee has a right to _____ in the workplace.

24. Employers must give information that _____ the employee to do his or her job.

25. If the firm _____ any kind of behavior in the workplace, they must tell employees.

26. No employee should have to tolerate being sexually _____ on the job.

27. Employers must notify employees regarding the _____ for filing a grievance.

28. Federal law protects a _____ disciplinary process at work.

29. Employees are entitled to reasonable job _____.

30. By law, managers must make job _____ clear.

Success with Law Words

Answer Key

1. freedom from doubt or anxiety
2. to recognize and accept
3. seclusion from the intrusion of others
4. information about the result of a process
5. to supply with the means to do something
6. to say no
7. to bother
8. to forbid
9. to agree to
10. a hope for the future
11. correct and standard procedure
12. complaint made by employee to management
13. working by degrees
14. unbiased
15. policies
16. refuse
17. feedback
18. impartial
19. grievance
20. honor
21. guidelines
22. acquiesce
23. privacy
24. enables
25. prohibits
26. harassed
27. protocol
28. progressive
29. security
30. expectations

Index

to abandon	81	to appear	105
to abate	57	to apply	65
absurd	105	to appoint	113
to abuse	109	arbitration	73
access	25	to arraign	33
to accompany	101	aspect	61
to accredit	61	assault	57
to accuse	77	assent	13
to acquiesce	117	to assert	61
to acquire	101	to assess	29
act	29	assets	113
action	13	to assign	21
actions	77	to assume	13
adequate	53	to assure	81
to adjust	93	to attract	85
administrator	113	authority	1
to advise	21	available	109
agency	1	to avow	9
agreement	9	to award	37
to allege	73	aware	17
to allot	69	to bar	73
to allow	97	to bargain	17
amount	109	to bear	17
to answer	45	(on someone's) behalf	5
to appeal	69	behavior	57

Success with Legal Words

beneficiary	113
to bind	9
body	1
bona fide	97
calculate	97
to cancel	109
capacity	29, 77
capital	85
case	29
category	9
casualty	97
to certify	69
characteristic	109
to charge	105
to check	49
circumstances	45
citation	105
claim	89
classification	29
clean slate	5
to coerce	113
to cohabitate	45
to collect	93
to command	69
commerce	101
to commit	77
to compare	109
to compel	9
to compensate	89
competent	9
complaint	29
to complete	69
complex	21
compromise	81
conditions	65
to conduct	49
conduct	57
conflict	81
confrontation	57
to consent	61
consequence	77
to consider	21
consistent	89
constitute	21
to consume	97
to contend	17
to consent	105
contract	21
contrary	45
to contribute	85
convenient	25
to convey	53

Index

to convict	33	depraved	77
cornerstone	53	to describe	89
to cover	65, 93	to designate	101
credit history	1	detail	89
creditor	41	to detain	77
criteria	65	determination	57
to cross-examine	33	to determine	93
custody	33	dire	93
custom	37	disapprove	57
damage	109	to discharge	5
to deal with	77	to discover	85
debt	41	to discriminate against	49
to deceive	85	to dismiss	105
to decide	29	dispute	41
decree	45	to disseminate	25
deduction	93	distance	29
to define	77	distinctive	101
to defraud	73	to distinguish	37
to delegate	1	to distribute	113
to deliberate	33	to divide	9
delinquent	77	to divulge	25
to deliver	13	to document	89
demand	89	to draw	93
to demonstrate	29	to elicit	1
to deny	25	to enable	117
to depend	65	to encompass	53

Success with Legal Words

to encourage	85	to file	5
to enforce	1	to fine	105
engagement	65	to fix	17
to enter	65	to force	81
to entitle	65	formal	17
to establish	17	foster care	37
to evaluate	25	to fund	93
to evict	81	garnish	41
to exercise	37	to gather	105
to exclude	109	goal	53
executor	113	goodwill	101
to exempt	97	to govern	65
to exhaust	5	to grant	25
to exist	17	grievance	117
expectations	117	gross	97
expense	53	grounds	45
to expire	109	to group	29
to explain	61	to guarantee	81
express	9	guardian	113
to extend	97	guidelines	117
extreme	5	habit	89
fact	17	to handle	49
factor	21	to harass	117
to favor	37	hazardous	25
feedback	117	heirs	113
to fail	21	hierarchy	21

Index

to hire	49	interview	49
to hold	65	intestate	113
to honor	117	to intimidate	57
hostile	57	intolerable	57
to identify	21	to intrude	81
to ignore	57	invent	85
impaired	61	to inventory	53
impartial	117	invest	97
implied	9	to investigate	109
impose	41	to involve	61
inappropriate	73	irreconcilable	45
incident	89	to issue	45
income	97	itemize	97
independent	73	to jeopardize	101
to influence	105	joint	37
informed	61	jurisdiction	45
to infringe	17	justice	9
ingrained	93	juvenile	77
to inherit	113	last resort	5
to initiate	113	leverage	17
injury	57	liable	5
innovation	85	to license	101
insolvent	93	limit	41
installment	25	living will	53
to intend	69	to maintain	69
to intervene	73	major	109

Success with Legal Words

mandatory	93	offer	9
manner	109	to omit	13
to manufacture	85	opportunity	89
material	17	to order	25
to mediate	81	origional	101
media	17	outline	37
method	53	outright	53
milestone	69	to own	53
minimum	49	paperwork	69
minor	25	to participate	61
misconduct	73	particular	97
misdemeanor	29	party	9
to modify	89	to pass	49
to monitor	101	penalty	1
to motivate	37	pending	85
motive	13	to perform	9
mutual	13	permanent	65
necessary	29	permission	61
notice	81	to pertain	1
notion	37	pervasive	57
to obey	73	to petition	37
to object	1	physical	89
obligations	5	plea	33
to obtain	73	policy	61
to occur	65	power	1
offense	77	power of attorney	53

Index

practical	81	prospective	49
practice	49	to protect	49
precaution	109	protocol	117
premises	81	prototype	85
premium	105	to prove	33
to prescribe	29	to provide	49
presence	33	provision	25
to preserve	53	public domain	21
to presume	17	public interest	45
to prevent	57	punctual	25
priority	37	punitive	73
privacy	117	to pursue	5
probable cause	29	qualification	49
probate	113	to qualify	93
procedure	5	to question	33
proceeds	41	quota	69
process	69	ramification	53
product	85	rare	5
proficient	69	reason	77
prognosis	61	reasonable	81
progressive	117	to receive	113
to prohibit	117	reciprocal	13
to project	93	reconcile	45
property	41	recover	41
to propose	5	to reduce	53
to prosecute	73	to refuse	117

Success with Legal Words

to refute	33	sale	85
regardless	61	sanction	1
to register	101	to satisfy	45
to regulate	25	scope	101
to rehabilitate	77	to screen	65
reliable	105	search	101
reluctant	37	secrecy	85
to remain	33	security	117
remedial	73	seize	41
to render	1	select	21
to renew	21	to serve	45
to repay	5	services	97
representative	113	settle	41
reputation	109	severity	105
to require	69	slogan	101
resolve	41	solemnity	13
responsible	57	source	97, 101
to restore	21		
restrict	41	speedy	33
to resume	45	to sponsor	69
return	93	stable	37
to review	1	to stand	33
to revoke	105	standard	41
right	49	to state	21
to risk	73	status	97
routine	61	strict	49

Index

subject	1	value	13
substantive	73	to vary	65
sue	41	victim	89
sufficient	13	to violate	81
suitable	37	voluntary	13
to sum up	33	to waive	69
to support	77	to warn	33
to suspend	105	warrant	29
to sustain	89	warranty	109
to swear	45	to weight	93
system	65	to withhold	13
to take into account	77	worth	13
tangible	17		
techniques	89		
term	81		
to terminate	1		
to track	105		
to transform	85		
treatment	61		
trustee	5		
understanding	9		
to undertake	13		
uniform	97		
use	101		
to utter	9		
valid	113		

About KAPLAN Educational Centers

Kaplan Educational Centers is one of the nation's premier education companies, providing individuals with a full range of resources to achieve their educational and career goals. Kaplan, celebrating its 60th anniversary, is a wholly-owned subsidiary of The Washington Post Company.

TEST PREPARATION & ADMISSIONS

Kaplan's nationally-recognized test prep courses cover more than 20 standardized tests, including entrance exams for secondary school, college and graduate school as well as foreign language and professional licensing exams. In addition, Kaplan offers private tutoring and comprehensive, one-to-one admissions and application advice for students applying to graduate school.

SCORE! EDUCATIONAL CENTERS

SCORE! after-school learning centers help students in grades K-8 build academic skills, confidence and goal-setting skills in a motivating, sports-oriented environment. Kids use a cutting-edge, interactive curriculum that continually assesses and adapts to their academic needs and learning style. Enthusiastic Academic Coaches serve as positive role models, creating a high-energy atmosphere where learning is exciting and fun for kids. With nearly 40 centers today, SCORE! continues to open new centers nationwide.

KAPLAN LEARNING SERVICES

Kaplan Learning Services provides customized assessment, education and training programs to K-12 schools, universities and businesses to help students and employees reach their educational and career goals.

KAPLAN INTERNATIONAL

Kaplan serves international students and professionals in the U.S. through Access America, a series of intensive English language programs, and LCP

International Institute, a leading provider of intensive English language programs at on-campus centers in California, Washington and New York. Kaplan and LCP offer specialized services to sponsors including placement at top American universities, fellowship management, academic monitoring and reporting and financial administration.

KAPLOAN

Students can get key information and advice about educational loans for college and graduate school through **KapLoan** (Kaplan Student Loan Information Program). Through an affiliation with one of the nation's largest student loan providers, **KapLoan** helps direct students and their families through the often bewildering financial aid process.

KAPLAN PUBLISHING

Kaplan Books, a joint imprint with Simon & Schuster, publishes books in test preparation, admissions, education, career development and life skills; Kaplan and *Newsweek* jointly publish the highly successful guides, **How to Get Into College** and **How to Choose a Career & Graduate School**. SCORE! and *Newsweek* have teamed up to publish **How to Help Your Child Suceed in School**.

Kaplan InterActive delivers award-winning, high quality educational products and services including Kaplan's best-selling **Higher Score** test-prep software and sites on the internet (**http://www.kaplan.com**) and America Online. Kaplan and Cendant Software are jointly developing, marketing and distributing educational software for the kindergarten through twelfth grade retail and school markets.

KAPLAN CAREER SERVICES

Kaplan helps students and graduates find jobs through Kaplan Career Services, the leading provider of career fairs in North America. The division includes **Crimson & Brown Associates**, the nation's leading diversity recruiting and publishing firm, and **The Lendman Group and Career Expo**, both of which help clients identify highly sought-after technical personnel and sales and marketing professionals.

COMMUNITY OUTREACH

Kaplan provides educational resources to thousands of financially disadvantaged students annually, working closely with educational institutions, not-for-profit groups, government agencies and other grass roots organizations on a variety of national and local support programs. Also, Kaplan centers enrich local communities by employing high school, college and graduate students, creating valuable work experiences for vast numbers of young people each year.

Paying for college just got easier...

KapLoan*, the Kaplan Student Loan Information Program, is a free service designed to guide you through the financial aid process.

KapLoan will send you a FREE booklet with valuable financial aid information and connect you with one of the nation's largest student loan providers. With KapLoan, you'll receive personalized guidance through the financial aid process and access to some of the least expensive educational loans available.

- **The Federal Stafford Loan**—Eligible students can borrow various amounts depending on their year in college. Loan amounts range from $2,625-$5,500 for dependent students and $6,625-$10,500 for independent students.
- **The Federal Parent Loan for Undergraduate Students (PLUS)**—Eligible parents may borrow up to the total cost of education, less other financial aid received.

Make the most of your financial aid opportunities.

KapLoan™
The Kaplan Student Loan Information Program

Contact KapLoan today!

1-888-KAP-LOAN
www.kaploan.com

*Kaplan is not a lender and does not participate in the determination of loan eligibility.
Calls made to 1-888-KAP-LOAN will be answered by a representative of a provider of federal and certain private educational loans.

LSAT*

9 Out of 10 Kaplan students get into one of their top-choice law schools.[†]

Competition for law school is tough, and your LSAT score can make all the difference. That's why you need to take Kaplan. For 60 years, we've helped more students get into law school than all other test prep companies combined. That's why we're the #1 choice for LSAT prep.

KAPLAN
1-800-KAP-TEST
www.kaplan.com

SIXTY · YEARS · OF · BUILDING · FUTURES

*LSAT is a registered trademark of the Law School Admission Council.
[†]1998 Bruskin-Goldring Research Study of students at the top 50 law schools.

Call or check out our web site to study anywhere in the U.S.